Your God-Gi[ven]
dreams are a[bout]
to take off!
[signature] Dix

Merry Christmas!
May you be inspired as
you read This book and
apply its principals.
Love, Terry Marsden Brasfield
Editor 2016

Jer. 29: 11-14

FLIGHT

Develop *Means* by Connecting *Wings* to God-Given Dreams

Amber Davis

Printed in the United States of America

First Printing 2016

ISBN-13 978-0-692-71638-0

Published by
A.W.I.P. A Work in Progress
Lebanon, TN

Cover design: Chad Davis, with photography: Glen Batson
Props for cover photo: *TinyLittleMinis*
Editing: Terry Brasfield
Interior design and typesetting: Carol Garcia

Author photograph by www.paulwharton.com

FLIGHT

Develop *Means* by Connecting *Wings* to God-Given Dreams

No matter what the dream, it takes a team.

Thank you first to God for His inspiration, encouragement, love, provision, and His faithfulness in taking this book to FLIGHT.

Thank you to my family. Years ago my husband, Chad and I began a journey of helping each other fulfill our God- given dreams. His love, support, encouragement, patience and prayers are a true gift to me. Our children, Abby Lu and Zeke, are the most amazing kids on the whole planet. I am so thankful to be in a family who values God-given dreams as well as the dedication it takes to fulfill them.

Terry Brasfield, what can I say? You are the most outstanding editor a writer could ever hope to have on her team! Thank you for your attention to detail, timeliness, communication, encouragement, skills – skills – skills, and more than any of these, your heart for FLIGHT. You are more than an editor; you are a friend of whom I truly value.

Thank you to FLIGHT designers and photography team: Carol Garcia, Chad Davis, and Glen Batson; your creativity and excellence is refreshing!

Thank you to Dr. Barry Brasfield, Twylla and Keith Foust, Jennifer Langford, Larry Dyke (Dad), Pastor Jim and Anne Frease, Bridget Rogers, Hayley DiMarco, Lisa Wilson, and Randy and Clare Rudder for your continued prayers, encouragement, wisdom, and support while this book has been taking to FLIGHT.

FLIGHT, the book, is much bigger than any one person could have produced. It is a noble cause to help others fulfill the plans God has placed in their hearts. I believe in you. I believe in the plans God has for each one of you and the dreams that he is calling you to fulfill. Thank you FLIGHT "Dream Team"! Thank you for believing that God can help us get from where we are to where He knows that we can be as we…

Develop *Means* by Connecting *Wings* to
God-Given Dreams

FLIGHT
Contents

"Let's Go For It!"

Our FLIGHT plans may never be as publicly
celebrated or investigated
as the likes of Charles Lindbergh
or Amelia Earhart.
They should at least be as equally anticipated
because they carry precious cargo:
God-Given Dreams

"Let's Go For It!"

Sporting starched business attire and tennis shoes, I was ready to enjoy a nap as I boarded a prop plane bound for the big city. I had just spent two weeks, of non-stop business, in a small farm town in western Missouri and was headed for another double week business trip to St. Louis. After ten straight days of long hours and no time for rest, I was looking forward to an hour nap accompanied by the hum of dual propellers.

The plane was full - all ten of us - and I was sleeping soundly before we even left the runway. Just outside of the city, I was awakened by turbulence and a child behind me mimicking crashing sounds. At that point in my life, I had been living on the road or in the air for a few years. I was pretty comfortable with the ups and downs of air transportation. However, the combination of bouncing around like a bobble head doll accompanied by Dennis the Menace with his repetitive hand gestures and voice-over of crash landings was trying to steal my peace. So, I began to lean forward to distance myself - if even an inch - from the sounds of the mini false prophet behind me, and that is when I overheard another conversation.

Not two inches in front of my face was the door to the cockpit, which was not a door but a wide piece of plaid fabric that hung down from what appeared to be shower curtain rings. On the other side of this plane tapestry were two pilots conversing with air traffic control. Amazingly, I could hear every word that they were speaking - even with the "security" curtain that flapped in between us. Air traffic control said something like:

"There are storms in the area around St. Louis; most flights have been diverted to (the dispatcher then gave the names of other cities). *There have been reports of funnel clouds with these storms. There are a few pockets between the clouds that you may be able to maneuver through. Let me know what you decide."*

The pilots gave a short pause. I was hanging onto every word and had shifted my body so that I could peer through where the curtain had gaped open so as to hear the conversation unfold. I saw one pilot look at the other - and then he said those four words that I never expected and would never forget:

"Let's go for it!"

I sat back, glared out my window, and tightened my seat belt. During this time in my life, I was a Christian, yet I had not been consistently walking (or flying) with the Lord. However, at that moment, I knew I needed God. I prayed for His favor as the plane banked left and, for all I knew, flew towards a "pocket" (that I hoped had the biggest hole in it that anyone had ever seen). I looked to my right and saw a black wall cloud and immediately turned to my left, looking past my colleague who was snoring through the whole adventure. That is when I saw another dark cloud moving into his window view.

The turbulence began to grow and several times the plane dropped altitude quickly. Then, over the intercom (which was just a parlor trick because with one swish of plaid to the left an intercom would not have been needed), the pilots told us that we might experience some turbulence during our descent. They assured us that it would be brief, and we would be on the ground soon. I liked "brief." However, considering I was privy to information that the other passengers were not, I did have concerns about what they defined as "on the ground soon."

It is never comforting to see lightning strike horizontally at your eye level.

The storm continued to increase in strength. When flying, it is not uncommon to drop vertically due to pockets of turbulence. However, you begin to take notice when the plane moves from side-to-side in quick bursts. I mustered up the courage (again) to look out my window and, to my delight, caught a glimpse of what appeared to be land illuminated by an electrical sky. I bowed my head and thanked God.

As I looked up, I noticed that we were slowly - yet very wobbly - approaching the earth. I did not have a pilot's license, but I knew that it was not the best landing approach for the plane's wings to act like a windmill. Suddenly the front of the plane and all of us in it leaned quickly forward and pulled to the right. Then - as fast as a finger-snap - the plane straightened up, and we were on the ground.

As soon as we hit the ground we took off, not in the air, but on the runway as if we were part of a high-speed chase. My sleeping co-worker awoke as I then tried to catch him up on the current events. We were thankfully interrupted by a pilot over the intercom saying something to the effect of:

"*Welcome to St. Louis. We are the only plane landing because there has been a tornado spotted near the airport. We are approaching the terminal, but the shuttles will not be in service* (the ones that are supposed to take you from the little planes to the main terminals). *Once we are to a safe site, we will deplane and get everyone to the airport terminal.*"

As we screeched around a turn and raced through the rain, I looked out my window again: all I saw was a black wall that encompassed the whole sky.

The plane came to a halt. The security curtain swished open. The pilots - as they opened the plane's door - instructed everyone to get their things, deplane quickly, and run to the airport stairwell door - a good fifty yards away.

So there I was - briefcase in one hand and purse strap wrapped around my neck - sprinting alongside the other members of our flight towards an international airport's terminal as a raging storm nipped at our heels. Once inside, we ran as fast as we could up several steps hoping to take a look at the storm from a safe place. It was then that we heard the loud crash of the tornado winds and the rain as it hit the big glass windows facing the tarmacs. As we opened the stairwell door and made our way into the boarding area, I heard one of the pilots say to the other:

"Thank God we made it!"

Pre-FLIGHT

From "*Let's go for it!*" to "*Thank God we made it!*" those pilots got from "where they were" to "where they needed to be." They had a dream - a dream to get to their destination. This dream that I am referring to was not their life-long destiny dream; this dream was to get a small plane and a few passengers from a county airport to a metro landing strip. This dream was to claim victory over a storm and arrive safely at their next stop. This dream was a connector: a connector to their next dream destination.

A life-long God-given dream is an amazing discovery. There are many great books that can inspire us to discover our life-long destinies, but this is not such a book. However, this book can help us arrive at those discovered destinies - one God-given dream at a time.

Our lives are made up of many God-given dreams or destinations. As we arrive at each one, we travel closer to our destiny. Knowing this, the question for many of us becomes: "How can I fulfill my current God-given dream - leading me to the next connection towards my destiny?" This book - FLIGHT - is just what you have been looking for if you find yourself asking this question.

"Okay then, what does the term FLIGHT mean?" I am glad that you asked because, for the next several chapters, we will embark on the *Means* of FLIGHT. The term FLIGHT is just that: the *Means*.

Means: what we are able to do with what we possess (abilities)[1]

We are given the *Means* - abilities - by which to accomplish our God-given dreams. We have the responsibility to develop these *Means* so that we can fulfill our God-given *dreams.*

"Now finish the work, so that your eager willingness to do it may be matched by your completion of it, according to your <u>means</u>. For if the willingness is there, the gift is acceptable according to what one has, not according to what one does not have."
(2 Cor. 8:11-12 NIV)

God has placed dreams and *Means* inside each of us. A dream, based on one definition, is a wish that is fully satisfied. Have you ever wished for a new car, a new job, or a new house? Or, how about this, have you ever wished that your proposal would be the one selected or that your parents would have an amazing fiftieth wedding anniversary? Have you ever wished you could graduate from school, write a novel, redecorate your bedroom, or simply reorganize your garage? Just like those pilots, it took more than a wish for them to arrive at their destination. For them to arrive, they had to make a connection between their *Means* and their God-given dreams.

"What is the connection between *Means* and God-given dreams?" That is a great question! Over our lifetime, God deposits multiple dreams in each of our hearts. Within those dreams, He gives us plans and ideas.

"For I know the plans I have for you," declares the Lord, "plans to prosper you and not to harm you, plans to give you hope and a future." (Jer. 29:11 NIV)

God has plans for each one of us. God deposits those plans inside the ideas that make up our dreams. When we seek "The One" who gives us those plans, we can begin to make the connection between our *Means* and our God-given dreams.

Not understanding this important connection has limited many from fulfilling the promises spoken by Jeremiah. It sure did limit me. The journey that has led me to write this book called FLIGHT has been a personal one.

While in college, I studied one of my passions - organizational communications, which led to a position as an assistant director for a non-profit organization. During college and this period of employment, I moonlighted with a restaurant company. After employment with the non-profit, I pitched a proposal to the restaurant company. I would travel and train, organize, plan, and develop in any area that they needed help - for little pay - as long as they would cover my travel and living expenses. They agreed. I soon began a life of living in airplanes and hotel rooms, experiencing many actual flights such as the true story, "*Let's Go For It!*" The experience I acquired along the way led to another company that hired me as an internal consultant. For several years, I lived my life among my clients traveling city to city and advising owners, managers, and staffs on how to get the most productivity from their employees. I had made a successful career out of something I was passionate about; yet, the dreams God had put in my heart were still waiting to get out.

I tell you this to let you know that although I was climbing the corporate ladder of success rather quickly, I had yet to make the connection between developing *Means* and fulfilling God-given dreams. I wanted to fulfill my God-given dreams - I just did not know how. For this reason, I kept busy doing what came easy and seemed to get me status and titles that I thought were fulfilling. They were not. Inside, I wanted more. Deep down, I knew that God had something better for me than what I was doing. But, I did not know how to go from where I was to get to where God knew that I could be. I had not made the connection between God's promises and developing the *Means* or abilities He had given me to fulfill my God-given dreams.

Wings: His God-breathed Word

The Word of God is packed with lifting power just waiting to be accessed by a person willing to go the distance. Many do not know how to connect God's Word to their God-given dreams. I was one of those people. Then, I discovered not only the lifting power of God's Word, but how to apply it - which equipped me to finish the work God had planned for me. This connection would eventually give lift to every dream He put in my heart.

FLIGHT is the culmination of the amazing revelation of the connection between *Means*, *Wings*, and God-given dreams.

Once we make that connection - once we are willing to say and act upon the words "*Let's go for it!*" and allow God's Word to develop the *Means* (the abilities that we already possess) - there is nothing that can stop us from fulfilling our God-given dreams.

Whether you feel accomplished or not, you may be in the same place I was - willing to pursue a life worth more than titles, status, or accomplishments - a life fulfilling the dreams inside of you.

Simply opening this book shows a willingness to go beyond our current location. But, it takes more than our willingness to begin. How do we develop and connect so as to fully satisfy those wishes we desire? No matter how big or small our God-given dreams, taking to FLIGHT can help us fulfill them. Our jobs, our homes, our churches, our families, our lives are just waiting for us to say "*Let's go for it!*" and finish the work God has for us. Then, we can say (with passion and not exhaustion), "*Thank God we made it!*" Because, as we develop and fulfill each God-given dream, we make the connection to the next dream God has in line towards fulfilling our destiny.

So come along, let's take a trip. It is time to…

Develop *Means* by Connecting *Wings* to God-Given Dreams

FLIGHT Plan

I had never been in an airport tower. So, you can imagine my excitement as my family and I crossed through the security gate and parked at the base of one of the busiest air traffic control towers in America. Blessed with the opportunity for a private walk-through, we began our tour in the radar room.

What stood out the most was the phraseology - it was here that we received a lesson in the language of air traffic. Approach radar controllers (trafficking takeoff or landing) relied on the specific language used by air traffic to fulfill their mission of "Safety First." With multiple plane icons appearing and disappearing from their screens, these amazing workers had to be speedy and accurate in communicating to their team members, as well as the pilots they guided. Their unique language filled the dark, quiet space as I stood in amazement listening to their foreign communication.

After leaving the radar room, we headed to the top floor of the tower where we could see beyond the small screens. And a tower it was: standing 150-feet high! After enjoying the journey of an elevator, stairs, and tight passageways, we arrived and opened a small gate. We stepped into a room surrounded by a series of outward slanted windows - each the size of French doors. Turning around a full 360 degrees, we were amazed by our unobstructed view. Our guide pointed out visible landmarks that gave us a sense of direction. It almost looked like a screen shot from a satellite map only clearer. Planes lit up the night sky. Our guide pointed to two planes arriving from the south as our heads spun to see many other planes taking off around us. The little icons we had seen in the radar room were now flying at eye level.

To ensure that air traffic continued to move, the tower and radar controllers kept their communication to the pilots and ground crews very short. Knowing and utilizing a common language helped both the pilots and ground crews communicate quickly and effectively. If everyone did not speak the same language, the safety of passengers and personnel would be compromised, and it would be very challenging for any flight to make it to its destination.

Phraseology helps put plans into action. Words can bring understanding. Whether we are working in a tower or learning how to fulfill our God-given dreams, it is important to speak the same language. Compared to the language of air traffic control, FLIGHT phraseology is quite simple.

Formulate: to put into a systematic statement or expression[1]

We must not only be able to imagine a dream, but we must also be able to express it. Formulating a dream may seem rigid (and even contrary to what dreaming is all about), but the inability to formulate a dream is what hinders most dreamers from seeing their dreams turn into realities. Formulating helps us close the distance between the words, *"Let's go for it!"* and *"Thank God we made it!"*

The *Means* of FLIGHT

During the Pre-FLIGHT section of this book, we defined FLIGHT as the *Means* expressed in Scripture in ***2 Corinthians 8:11-12***. We then defined the word *Means* as abilities or what we are able to do with what we possess. The *Means* of FLIGHT is an acronym for:

F ORWARD THINKING

L INK ACTIONS TO IDEAS

I NVOLVE THOSE NEEDED

G ENERATE A PLAN

H AVE ACCOUNTABILITY

T HANKSGIVING

Departures and Arrivals

To better understand this acronym, it is important to know <u>when</u> we should begin to develop the *Means* of FLIGHT. Any good system or process has a beginning, middle, and end - in other words, departure and arrival times. In FLIGHT terms, we will call these times: ***A Time to Create***, ***A Time to Generate***, and ***A Time to Celebrate***. These three "times" help us group the *Means* of FLIGHT. This way, we do not become overwhelmed by all of our development. We can simply take it one departure and arrival at a time.

Great! Sounds like a plan, right? Not quite. Our FLIGHT Plan would be nothing without these next important components.

Connector Questions and Gate #s

I do not remember what airport I was in, but I remember vividly a time when I quickly changed gates to avoid a huge detour. I was overseas in an international airport, traveling with a few business colleagues when we decided to set our luggage down in front of what we thought was our connector gate. A little jetlagged and with no seating available, some of us sat down on the floor and closed our eyes. A few moments passed, and we looked up to see armed guards speaking in Turkish around us. That is when we noticed that we had lined up at the gate for Istanbul - instead of our USA destination. Moments away from a Visa status check, we gathered our belongings and made our way to our correct connector gate. Had we made the wrong connection, we would have denied ourselves the joy of making it to our desired destination and would have experienced, I am sure, many more challenges.

Connectors are like questions: when we choose or ask the right ones, we arrive where we need to be. We develop the *Means* of FLIGHT when we ask the right questions along the way. Each *Means* of FLIGHT has one or two questions that, when answered, helps us develop the *Means* to connect to our next gate. If we look at these questions as a gate to our next development, we can enjoy asking the right questions because we know that the answers that come from them ultimately help us arrive at our dream destination. However, simply asking the right questions is not enough. There is work involved to develop *Means.*

Maneuvers and Maintenance

Maneuvers are what we should do while Maintenance is how to do what will help us maneuver through.

Maneuvers and Maintenance help us develop the *Means* of FLIGHT by giving us specifics that we can work on before, during, and even after we have arrived at our destinations. It is through the work that we develop. However, work alone will not take our God-given dreams to FLIGHT.

Wings

We develop *Means* by connecting *Wings* to God-given dreams. The *Means* of FLIGHT - with its departure and arrival times, Connector Questions and Gate #s, and Maneuvers and Maintenance - must be connected to *Wings* in order to take to FLIGHT. *Wings* bring lift to our development. Without lift, we may see some success, but we will not fulfill the plans God has for us. Through FLIGHT, we will learn how God lifts us with **passion, perseverance**, and **people** - giving us revelation through **planning** and **productivity** - while bringing **pleasure**.

This phraseology helps our FLIGHT Plan come together. Our FLIGHT Plan is made clearer with the development of each *Means* of FLIGHT. Each chapter of FLIGHT takes a closer look at this Plan. Working our FLIGHT Plan will help us make the right connections as well as, *"Now finish the work!"* But, what happens when the work is finished?

In-FLIGHT Check

Recording what we learn along the way will help us develop beyond today!

Our FLIGHT Plan builds on each chapter and ends with an In-FLIGHT Check. This In-FLIGHT Check helps us keep a record of our answers to the Connector Questions and Gate #s. This Check also helps us keep the *Wings* - those Scriptures that we have a personal connection with - written out so that we continually stay lifted. Recording what we learn along the way will help us in the pursuit of our current God-given dream as well as future God-given dreams. With each destination, we should be able to apply what we have learned from the previous one: getting better and growing along the way.

FLIGHT Pattern and FLIGHT at a Glance

We should notice a pattern when we apply what we have learned each time we take a God-given dream to FLIGHT. In the "Thank God we made it!" section of this book we learn the importance of reapplying this FLIGHT Pattern to each God-given dream. This section also gives us FLIGHT at a Glance - a grid outlining the details of our FLIGHT Plan which will help us remember the *Means* and phraseology of FLIGHT.

Knowing the definitions of the *Means* of FLIGHT is just the beginning to help us get to where God knows that we can be. Learning takes a lifetime, so I do not pretend to tell you that, after reading this book, any of us will have developed all the *Means* to fulfill our God-given dreams. But with each dream, we grow and develop the *Means* of FLIGHT as we travel from destination to destination.

"Let's go for it!" because we cannot get to where God knows that we can be until we begin to...

Develop *Means* by Connecting *Wings* to God-Given Dreams

For reapplication use printable versions
of the In-FLIGHT Check pages,
go to the link below to access these and other resources:

www.yourflightplans.com/tools

A Time to Create

Create: to grow, invest, and to bring into existence[1]

To create, we must bring something from somewhere. If someone asks us to bring something, they must know that we already possess it. For this reason, bringing it means we must actively go get it. God created dreams and placed them on the inside of us. Our part is to allow God to help us creatively think and link our dreams to actionable steps so as to fulfill them.

A Time to Create is the time when we should seek out the **passion** and **perseverance** that God has created for us so that we can bring forth and fulfill the dreams He has placed in us. How do we do this? It begins by developing the *Means* of FORWARD THINKING and LINK ACTIONS TO IDEAS.

Chapter One

FORWARD THINKING

"So, what does it look like?" I asked as my colleague tried to describe the movie set to me. She explained that it was looking more and more like an airport every day. Weeks before, three internal consultants with a well-known food service company met to decide which one of us would be the "best fit" to travel to Hollywood, California, and help carry the vision for our company. With me pregnant and another preparing for a trip to Asia, the decision was easy. Although only one of us could actively participate in this project, our whole department enjoyed being involved and kept in touch through phone calls and emails.

The need seemed simple: be on set to help the designers create a replica of one of our company's stores. However, this was more than a set. This replica was to be one of the most expensive sets ever built for a movie. The director decided to forego the cost and challenges of shooting in an actual airport and, instead, decided to build one. To make the airport more believable, popular food court or shopping mall companies fought for or were asked to place their precious products in faux stores within the set itself. The inclusion of these companies created the need for consultants, representing their companies, to be there for guidance, ideas, and direction.

The dream was almost too big to imagine! My co-worker's attention was not on the airport itself; instead, her role was to keep the focus on and within the four walls of our company's store. She could not concern herself with what the other "pretend shops" were looking like (other companies had different design contracts establishing how real their models should appear). It was her job to stick with our company's plan as it was connected to the bigger picture.

With each phone call, my co-worker would tell me how amazingly real the director's vision was progressing. At the time, all three of us were working on multiple projects. We were sure that the director was also working on many other productions, knowing that he was very sought after and had many businesses to oversee. I remember thinking how all of our productivity helped to complete several little dreams simultaneously.

Upon the arrival home of one-third of our trio, we rejoiced with her that she had gotten to be part of such a fun assignment. Later, when that movie was released in the theaters, our company's model was briefly seen. The airport's hustle and bustle of people trying to make their connections merely complimented the make-believe world the producers had created. It could have seemed like a lot of effort for very little exposure. But to those involved, the pleasure came from pursuing and helping to fulfill what seemed to be an impossible dream.

I have always been more of a planner than a dreamer. With God supplying the dream, it has helped take the pressure off of me. Our itineraries could not exist if it were not for the destinations: otherwise, what would be the point? Everything required - from timelines to connectors, to the people involved, to the funds assigned - directs the outcome of the dream. As long as the dreams are from God, He will give us the **passion** and **perseverance** needed to accomplish them.

The focus of FLIGHT is not in the dreaming but more about the fulfilling of the dreams that God has given us. Just like my colleague and those involved with that movie set, we must stay focused on the God-given dream we have been asked to help fulfill. Asking the right questions helps us focus on developing the *Means* of where we are, as well as helps us connect to where we need to be. However, before we begin making connections, it is important to clarify our destination. For this reason, the first question we ask before taking FLIGHT is:

Gate #1 - CONNECTOR QUESTION
"What is the dream and what is the point of that dream?"

Maneuver: Discover the Destination

Whether we are overseeing a movie set production or a five-year- old child's birthday party, at some point we should have discovered that this was the dream that God had for us to pursue.

Dreams can seem complicated, but, thank God, He helps us keep it simple. Discover the Destination is as easy as one, two, three.

Maintenance: Three R's to Remember Respect, Return, Reinforce

1. **Respect**: Begin by being thankful and expectant

God created us to succeed - not to fail, so why do so many dreams fail? I think this is an important question to consider. I will spend more time on this in the THANKSGIVING chapter, but there is something that I would like to address here in the beginning stages of FLIGHT: the word "thankful."

When we start to take to FLIGHT, we must check our "thank tank" and begin to develop it to a full level. If we thank ourselves *first*, before thinking to thank "The One" who gave us the dream, we will set ourselves and our dreams up for failure. Starting out thankful and expectant will create a great environment for us to more easily to receive direction, help, guidance, correction, and favor. For this reason, I will, from here on, refer to this word as "thank-full."

Being thank-full is a matter of what fills our hearts. When we are thank-full, we will say "thank you." But, just because we speak words of thanks does not make us full of it - of thanks, I mean.

When we are thank-full, we are stuffed with humility, meekness, and gratitude; there is no room for pride or status.

While this should be obvious, it was not to me. For years, I was full of other things like self-worth and pride. At the time, I thought that I was thank-full. But, as I look back, deep down I thought that I was a self-made woman.

So what are the best ways to fill up our "thank tanks" so that we can take to FLIGHT? I do not have all the answers, but here are some ideas that I have learned from the Bible on how to "Fill 'er up!" on thanks.

Upon waking, we should begin each morning by thanking God for giving us people, ideas, concepts, possessions, provisions, and, most importantly, His love. The book of Psalms is a collection of songs, poems, and heartfelt, thank-full prayers. Reading and speaking thank-full prayers puts us in a mindset that starts our day focused on being thank-full. Such discipline also helps to remind us that we have nothing to do with the fact that we have all of these wonderful things, ideas, and concepts. We will begin to see that we have these things simply because God *so* loves us, and He wants to bless us.

Throughout each day, we should remember to say the words "Praise God" or "Thank you, God" when even the smallest blessings come our way. Remember, we are reprogramming and fueling our "thank tanks" by a different and powerful source. Speaking thank-full words reminds us of the recipient of our thanks - God.

Depending on where we are in our development, we may

need to speak thank-full words often - to overhaul our thoughts - to position ourselves to take to FLIGHT. Speaking words of thanks might feel strange or even over the top. But, think on this: how "goodly" ("badly" need not apply when it comes to God-given dreams) do we want to fulfill the dreams God has given to us? Our gauge on this question will help determine what we are willing to do - or say - to get our God-given dream off the ground.

2. **Return**: Dreams worth seeking

Have you ever wondered, "What if I miss God's plan for my life?" I know I have. But, I discovered that - one of the greatest things about God is - He wants us to fulfill our dreams more than we do!

Identifying God-given dreams may be as easy as paying attention to the dreams that continue to pop-up in our hearts. My pastor, Pastor Jim Frease of Joy Church International - the biggest dreamer that I know - explains God-given dreams in an unforgettable way. Imagine the dream God has for us as a beach ball. When we push that beach ball down into the water, what will it eventually do? You've got it! That ball will continually pop back up every time. That is the same as God's dream in our hearts.[1]

But, what if I mistake that beach ball for a tether ball and get hit in the face with a dream that I created in my head instead of God's dream for my life? We must remember that God wants us to fulfill *His* dreams, and He will help us identify the dreams that He has placed inside of us instead of us being fooled by our own, self-generated dreams.

"For I know the plans I have for you," declares the Lord, "plans to prosper you and not to harm you, plans to give you hope and a future." (Jer. 29:11 NIV)

God has plans for us. All planners know (and all non-planners have witnessed) the passion of someone who has plans. God is no different. He created us for a specific purpose. So I had to ask myself, "Why would my Creator, who also has designed a specific purpose for me, not work with me to help me fulfill His plans?" God knows to whom He gives His dreams. He loves us just the way we are, but He is willing to help us get to where He *knows* that we can be! As we incline our ears towards the Lord, He will show us where to go and how to get there. None of us are perfect; but, as we develop and discover the dreams that God has placed inside of us, we can prepare to take to FLIGHT.

3. **Reinforce**: A dream should never be forced

Many people that I have encountered, including myself, have tried forcing a dream. I cannot speak for those people, but I can tell you my story. Several years ago, my husband and I came across a great business opportunity. We spent time calculating the cost and surrounding ourselves with others who had seen success in similar businesses. The one thing that we did not do was seek God and *listen.*

At the time, we thought that because we prayed for our business, we had involved God. But, what we had done was grabbed an opportunity that was not God's plan for our lives. Now, God is a good God and ***"His mercy endureth for ever" (Psalm 118:1 KJV)*** - Hallelujah! But we had chosen this decision and for this reason, we accumulated unwanted debt and many relationships based on works. After several years of forcing our business to produce fruit, we finally got honest with God - and ourselves - and humbly asked Him for forgiveness and clear direction.

When my husband came to me, after much time with the Lord, and told me that we needed to close up shop, I wrestled with many emotions. One thing I do not like is quitting. I am a bit of a competitor and my first response was, "How can we quit?" Deep down, I knew what we had to do, but I did not want to give up. One of the struggles in forcing a dream is, at some point, it will force you to do what you never dreamed of doing. We had to make a choice: quit the vision that we started on our own or quit the dream that God intended for us to begin in the first place. Facing such a decision is never fun or easy, but we knew what we had to do.

Although we had made choices that put us into an uncomfortable position, God was with us the whole time - even through the tough conversations. You see, when you force a vision, it has a ripple effect - impacting the lives of others. It is true that your dream is never just yours. We could have just closed down and hid under a rock (and that thought did cross my mind), but we knew that we had to confront the situation directly. This time of our lives was not the most enjoyable, but God stood with us in those hard times.

I share this story to encourage you to seek God *first* and to not rush to make a dream decision based on what seems to be working for someone else. There are so many wonderful opportunities in this world that we could mistake as our destiny, but God has a specific purpose for each of us. None of us are perfect, but - when we seek godly counsel - we can learn from "The One" who is without mistakes.

Forcing a dream causes instability. If, however, we can tie our life to a dream that God has created, then we can reinforce it and soar higher than we ever expected. I truly believe that God has already created a great work for us; all we have to do is find out what it is and live the rest of our lives reinforcing it.

Reinforce: to strengthen by additional assistance, support; to make stronger; to increase by fresh additions; to stimulate; to encourage[2]

One of the best ways to reinforce a dream is to write it out and put it up.[3] Write it in a frequented planner, magnetize it to the fridge, dry erase it on a bathroom mirror, tape it to the wall next to a nightstand, or Velcro it on the dashboard of the car; whatever it takes to reinforce it, do it! When we see something, we are stimulated. When we read it out loud, we are encouraged.

These two key forms of reinforcement help to keep our God-given dreams strong as we take them to FLIGHT. God knows the plans He has for us; He wants us to know that we know them, too.

God is in our corner - cheering us on, coaching us along, and reminding us that we can finish what we start. When we choose to work towards a God-given dream, we will develop confidence in Him. Rooted in God, we will confidently be more apt to recognize the dreams He plants in our hearts and able to pursue those dreams with both **passion** and **perseverance**. Once we recognize a God-given dream, God will help us to fulfill it.

Gate #2 - CONNECTOR QUESTION
"How do I motivate and measure my God-given dream?"

We should never go beyond FORWARD THINKING until we believe that our God-given dream will succeed. If we do not believe in our God-given dream, why would anyone else? Beyond this point, we should think in terms of our dream as a destination and not a "guestimation." What I mean is that we should use words that *lift* our dream. We should fuel our dream so that it has every opportunity to take FLIGHT. It would be very disconcerting if we heard a pilot say, "Well *if* we make it, this is what will happen." Our God-given dream carries precious cargo - our destiny; so, whatever we do, we should be resolute about taking that God-given dream to FLIGHT.

Once we have made the decision that our God-given dream is our destination, we must be able to measure the success of our trip. Measuring our success will help us develop the *Means* to apply towards our next God-given dream. Then, how do we set and read our gauges so that our FLIGHT does not get off course?

Maneuver: Measure it so that we can treasure it

I enjoy writing, planning, organizing, and communicating. But, when it comes to measuring, I must admit that I usually don't get too excited - that is until God served it to me in a special way. One of my favorite Scriptures is ***2 Corinthians 8:11-12***. These verses were, in fact, the inspiration for my writing this book. In addition to the wisdom gained from these verses, God has been able to use these verses to simplify the subject of measurement.

"Now finish the work, so that your eager willingness to do it may be matched by your completion of it, according to your <u>means</u>. For if the willingness is there, the gift is acceptable according to what one has, not according to what one does not have."
(2 Cor. 8:11-12 NIV)

Maintenance: "*Now finish the work!*"

These four words can change a person's life. Each word is powerful in and of itself. I could write a whole book about these four words, but I simply want to describe them individually. The word "now" means…now, not tomorrow. Coupling this present time request with the direction to "finish" will help us reach our destination. The word "the" is very important. God chose "the" instead of "your" to emphasize that we are to finish what He has already begun, not what we are about to start. The word "work" implies that there is some action to take for us to make it to our destination.

Based on these four words, measuring is simply being able to know that we have finished the work. We can measure our dream by the dream itself. The fulfillment of the dream signals its completion.

Is it that simple? Yes and no. Measuring a dream is a process: to fulfill our dream, we must make the connectors along the way. Taking to FLIGHT is designed to help us map out those connectors so that we can reach our destinations. In each chapter of FLIGHT, we can challenge ourselves with these four words - "*Now finish the work!*" - before moving on to the next Connector Question. God's directive to "*Now finish the work!*" sets the gauge for each *Means* of FLIGHT. If we are completing the work along the way, then we are on track to arrive at our destination.

"*Now finish the work!*" gives us "focus" so that we can see our destination. This focus fuels our **passion** and **perseverance** as we begin taking our God-given dreams to FLIGHT. If my colleague had focused on the other people's dreams on that movie set she would have gotten distracted, causing her to waste the energy needed to finish her assignment. In other words, the *Means* of her FLIGHT would have had to stop to refuel, causing her a delayed arrival at her destination.

In addition to focusing on our God-given dream, we must not become overwhelmed with how to start what we have discovered we must finish. When we keep our focus on "*Now finish the work!*" instead of getting bogged down in how to begin, we develop the *Means* of FORWARD THINKING. As we focus on the work, we will begin to treasure our God-given dream. When we treasure a dream, we can measure a dream (no matter how big or small we think that it may be).

Let's review. In FORWARD THINKING, we have passed through two very important gates by asking two very important questions. Along with their Maneuvers and Maintenance, these questions will help us develop the *Means* to fulfill our God-given dream.

FORWARD THINKING

Gate #1 - CONNECTOR QUESTION

"What is the dream and what is the point of that dream?"

Maneuver: Discover the Destination

Maintenance: Three R's to Remember Respect, Return, Reinforce

1. **Respect**: Begin by being thankful and expectant
2. **Return**: Dreams worth seeking
3. **Reinforce**: A dream should never be forced

Gate #2 - CONNECTOR QUESTION

"How do I motivate and measure my God-given dream?"

Maneuver: Measure it so that we can treasure it

Maintenance: *"Now finish the work!"*

FORWARD THINKING has helped us to recognize and know - with confidence - our God-given dream. Now, we are ready to take our God-given dream to FLIGHT as we move from FORWARD THINKING to LINK ACTIONS TO IDEAS. However, before we move on to our next *Means* of FLIGHT, we will do an In-FLIGHT Check. Writing down answers to our Connector Questions and our Scriptures that ignite **passion** and **perseverance** will help us…

Develop *Means* by Connecting *Wings* to God-Given Dreams

In-FLIGHT Check

Recording what we learn along the way will help us develop beyond today!

Develop *Means* of FORWARD THINKING by answering this Connector Question: "What is the dream and what is the point of that dream?"

____
____
____
____

Connecting *Wings* of **passion** and **perseverance**: Seek God and write out Scriptures that lift the answer to the above question.

____
____
____
____

Develop *Means* of FORWARD THINKING by answering this Connector Question: "How do I motivate and measure my God-given dream?"

____
____
____
____

Connecting *Wings* of **passion** and **perseverance**: Seek God and write out Scriptures that lift the answer to the above question.

____
____
____
____

Buckle up. The *Means* of FLIGHT are about to takeoff!

For reapplication use printable versions
of the In-FLIGHT Check pages,
go to the link below to access these and other resources:

www.yourflightplans.com/tools

Chapter Two

LINK ACTIONS TO IDEAS

I do not recall where I was traveling to, but I do remember that day of flying and how God changed my way of thinking about setting and completing goals. During that flight, when I made my next connector, I paid close attention to the ascending, cruising, and descending moments. Something about those three stages of that flight spoke to me.

That day, I realized we can all become thrilled and excited about soaring to new heights with our dreams; but, unless we get specific about how to land, we will never reach our destination. Being above reality - in the air, soaring with wings as eagles - is an amazing place to be. Yet, even a divine bird needs to land. Specific things must take place to make that happen. Then it occurred to me: let our God-given dreams soar, but "*Bring it to the Hangar!*" when it comes to the ideas attached to them.

On the same flight that I discovered the "*Bring it to the Hangar!*" phrase, I became equally intrigued with the metaphor of the "*Takeoff!*" I noticed that as the plane left the ground and ascended into the sky above the clouds I became excited, anxious, nervous, yet full of anticipation. Once the plane reached a cruising altitude, however, I noticed I became calm and peaceful, anticipating an easy ride. I then got a vision of what took place on the ground which resulted in such an enjoyable flight.

I became aware of the importance of both taking off and landing - not only for a plane but for personal development. The specifics of what was accomplished in the hangar directly affected how the flight was able to fulfill its course. How the flight was able to fulfill its course directly affected what was then to be accomplished in the hangar during the next connection. Although commercial airlines may not use hangars between each connector, this example still applies with or without the actual hangar building. The point is - there is always a need for maintenance on the ground. I did not know it at the time, but this vision of actions, ideas, and the specifics that link them together was more than just a thought in flight but a dream taking FLIGHT.

Developing the *Means* of FLIGHT begins with a dream. The ideas God gives us along the way help us set goals that critically link the dream to ground-level actions leading to productivity. Without goals, our dreams will remain "up in the air" and our ground-level actions will never take to FLIGHT. Once we know the dream, then God will give us the ideas. It is our responsibility to do something with those ideas. LINK ACTIONS TO IDEAS is truly ***A Time to Create*** and the groundwork for the itinerary that will help us take to FLIGHT.

LINK ACTIONS TO IDEAS, simply put, means to be *Creatively Specific* when it comes to the dreams that God has given us. Having this traveling skill positions us to be a person of action and helps eliminate vague goals. Active people apply **passion** and **perseverance** to whatever they pursue. God will lift a person who takes action in the right direction. When God gives us a dream and fills that dream with ideas, He will help us put those ideas into action in a *Creatively Specific* way.

Creatively Specific: tying details to ideas

When I think of being *Creatively Specific*, I cannot help but remember the story of Jacob from the Scriptures. Jacob was not perfect, but he was a man who learned to seek God so that He could arrive at his dream destination. Jacob had a God-given dream to take possession of a land that, at the time, he was leaving. If he had stayed where he was and admired the land that was to be given to him, he would never have received it.[1]

Jacob was not able to wrap his head around how that God-given dream was going to become a reality. Instead of focusing on the dream, he did something that was so powerful: Jacob moved forward and trusted God.

God continued to give Jacob connector dreams along the way to the big dream He had planned for him. Dreams - like who to marry and how to succeed in business - were placed in Jacob's heart accompanied with the ideas for how to fulfill them. Jacob thought *Creatively Specific* thoughts and took action as he began developing the *Means* of how to LINK ACTIONS TO IDEAS. Each idea linked to actions helped fulfill these connector dreams until - over time - he arrived at the ultimate destination God had planned for him. Jacob's ideas are some of the most *Creatively Specific* ideas ever written.

One of the ideas that God gave Jacob helped him and his father-in-law employer divide their livestock evenly. His idea became more and more creative and specific until his actions produced results. He was able to LINK ACTIONS TO IDEAS in a *Creatively Specific* way so that God then put the "super" onto his "natural" actions.[2]

You might be thinking, "That was great for Jacob, but I still do not know how to get the dream God gave me off of the ground." I have found when we focus on the dream, it is hard to take action; but, when we focus on the action, the dream will be fulfilled. God challenges us - to get moving! The *Means* of LINK ACTIONS TO IDEAS helps us do just that.

I believe that, just like Jacob, we all can develop the *Means* of LINK ACTIONS TO IDEAS and move forward the plans that God has for us. How can we do this? We can find this answer by asking two very important questions.

Gate #3 - CONNECTOR QUESTION
How do I land this plane *Creatively Specific*?

Maneuver: "*Bring it to the Hangar!*"

Before I get *Creatively Specific* about the phrase "*Bring it to the Hangar!*" let me explain a little more about the journey of how this phrase impacted many, including myself. Shortly after God placed the "*Bring it to the Hangar!*" phrase in my heart, I had the opportunity to teach planning and goal-setting to newly hired managers. I was eager to teach a subject for which I had passion. But, although I had been given a gift to teach and a gift for planning, the teacher became the student as I realized that did not mean I knew how to teach others to plan. One of the biggest mistakes that I made was trying to "give" people their goals instead of teaching them how to set goals based on God-given ideas.

Even though my technique of teaching was successful, there was still something missing. While the technique produced measurable, immediate results, its long-term application was not sustained. I am convinced that had we properly applied the right Maintenance before and after "*Bring it to the Hangar!*" we would have been more effective.

Maintenance: Pray, Speak, Link

Pray

It has taken me many years to realize that prayer should always be the "first step" towards reaching a dream. Prayer helps us be more specific regarding the dreams that God has placed in our hearts - because He, after all, is "The One" who put them there. Prayer alone is not enough. But prayer - based on the Word of God - gives lift to the *Means* of FLIGHT. No matter how powerful

I may think my words are, they do not compare to the Word of God. I have learned that when I pray I am to speak the words that are guaranteed to lift any God-given dream I am pursuing. Below is an example of a *Creatively Specific* prayer lifted by Scripture.

Father God, in the name of Jesus, I hear your voice, I increase in learning, and I am a person of understanding regarding what goals would help me to
(insert God-given dream HERE).[3]
I believe that I am blessed coming and going as I link actions to this dream you have given me.[4]
In Jesus name, Amen.

(This prayer is merely an example. It should help inspire us to dig into the Word of God for ourselves and discover Scriptures that speak directly to each one of our hearts and the dreams God has given us.)

God works through humble people to get things accomplished. When we humble ourselves and seek Him first, His Word promises that He will teach and guide us how we should do it. Once our pride is out of the way, God can help us get to where He knows that we can be.

Speak

Our words are important. I have known for a long time the importance of speaking a dream aloud. When we pray and give utterance to a dream and apply the "*Bring it to the Hangar!*" concept - we begin to see this dream in a whole new way. When bringing our dream "...*to the Hangar!*" we force our mind to think *Creatively Specific* as we explain that dream through ideas. Then we can tie those ideas to details, getting that dream on the ground to complete real actions.

"Bring it to the Hangar!" in Action

Now, I am going to ask you to do something that may seem silly and will most likely make you look quite stupid. Wow, who is ready to jump in with an introduction like that? Well, think about it this way: your reputation has probably been compromised by simply reading this book regardless, so why not go all in? I mean, you *are* reading a book called FLIGHT comprised of catchy acrostics and mega-metaphors. If it makes you feel any better, hundreds of managers of successful businesses have done what I am going to ask you to do.

If you feel a nudge of hesitation ask yourself, "Do I want to get to my destination or am I simply reading this book to pass the time?" Your answer will determine whether you participate; but, your participation (I promise you) will spark something inside of you that will get you closer to your destination.

Are you ready? Wow, what a buildup! What if I said that we were going to wait until the end of the book for you to do this great activity - would you be disappointed? Are you contemplating turning to the end of the last chapter to find out what it is? Great! That very anticipation is the excitement that will drive you to do it now. So, here we go!

Although reading the directions in advance is beneficial in most cases, doing so may stall you from participating, so just jump in.

Read each step, do it, and then move to the next step.

1. **Stand up, put your arms out to create a horizontal line, and do not close your eyes (you might fall over).**
2. **While keeping your arms out, think of your destination and say it out loud.**
3. **Still, in this same position, think of one idea related to your destination. If you are having trouble here (keep those arms up!), simply ask yourself, "What is one thing that must happen for me to reach my destination?" Your answer is an idea.**
4. **Speak that idea a second time; only this time - directly following speaking - sweep your hands down to your side (fingertips to thighs) and say the words, *"Bring it to the Hangar!"***
5. **Repeat the action a few times to let it sink in.**

I am not going to ask you if you feel like a fool, but you are probably wondering why you just imitated a bird in flight! I want to encourage you: I have seen amazing results come from this technique. Plus you already did it, so embrace it! The real question is, "Is this embarrassing moment seared into your memory?" I would venture to say that it is and, for this reason, "*Bring it to the Hangar!*" will become a thought process for goal setting that you will never forget. The first time someone follows the "*Bring it to the Hangar!*" action steps, they are usually not very specific in their details - this is to be expected. People tend to think and speak in generalities. The most successful people I know have developed the skill of being *Creatively Specific* - tying details to God-given ideas at a much quicker rate than the average person. Their success does not mean that everyone has or needs to be detail-oriented to fulfill a God-given dream. It does mean that all people should recognize the importance of details so they can either work on the details or oversee those who do.

Link

You see, every time we "*Bring it to the Hangar!*" we need to be able to answer two very important questions about that idea. The first question helps us to land the plane that will help get the dream God gave us down to a ground-level action. The second question…well, first things first…back to the first question. Landing the plane requires being *Creatively Specific.*

So, let me use an example. Let's keep it simple and relatable. God has blessed each one of us in so many ways; I would like to focus on one blessing that we all have in common. God has given each one of us a body to occupy. Beyond outward appearances, we all have a God-given desire to be healthy. I am not a nutritionist, doctor, or personal trainer; I am merely using the desire for a healthy body as an example because we can all relate to this God-given dream. The desire to have a healthy body is a general dream. But by applying the "*Bring it to the Hangar!*" action steps, we can personalize this dream and LINK ACTIONS TO IDEAS by thinking *Creatively Specific.*

Let's say that we have prayed and sought God in His Word regarding this dream of having a healthy body. Next, we stand with arms out and speak this dream out loud, "I have a healthy body." Note: when we speak in the present tense, our dream becomes a promise rather than a proclamation.

Let's assume that our God-given dream of "I have a healthy body" produced the idea that X% body fat would enable us to have the stamina and perseverance to pursue our other God-given dreams. Now this dream alone is not specific, but one question can help us tie it to details.

"What is one thing that must happen to fulfill this dream?"

Going one step further, let's say that we repeated this question until four different answers came to us. These answers are now ideas. These four ideas are:

* Eat Right * Exercise * Rest/Recreation * Education *

These ideas are great categorically but are still not *Creatively Specific* because they lack details. When we apply the "*Bring it to the Hangar!*" steps these four ideas become do-able actions that, if pursued, will help us fulfill our God-given dream.

By repeating the "*Bring it to the Hangar!*" steps with each of these four ideas we will…well, bring these ideas to the hangar. **We know we have arrived at "…*the Hangar!*" when we can put a**

date next to our answer. Once we do this, then we can complete or delegate each action. "*Bring it to the Hangar!*" in its simplest terms brings to mind a plane brought in not only for a landing but parked so that it can prepare to take to FLIGHT.

As we navigate each level and apply the "*Bring it to the Hangar!*" steps ask, "What is one thing that must happen to fulfill this dream?" We then move from the dream to ideas by asking, "What is one thing that must happen to fulfill this idea?" The following is a visual of what *"Bring it to the Hangar!"* looks like when using the above example.

"Bring it to the Hangar"

Remember, you are moving down when you "Bring it to the Hangar."
(Pray, Speak, Link)
This visual reads from top to bottom.

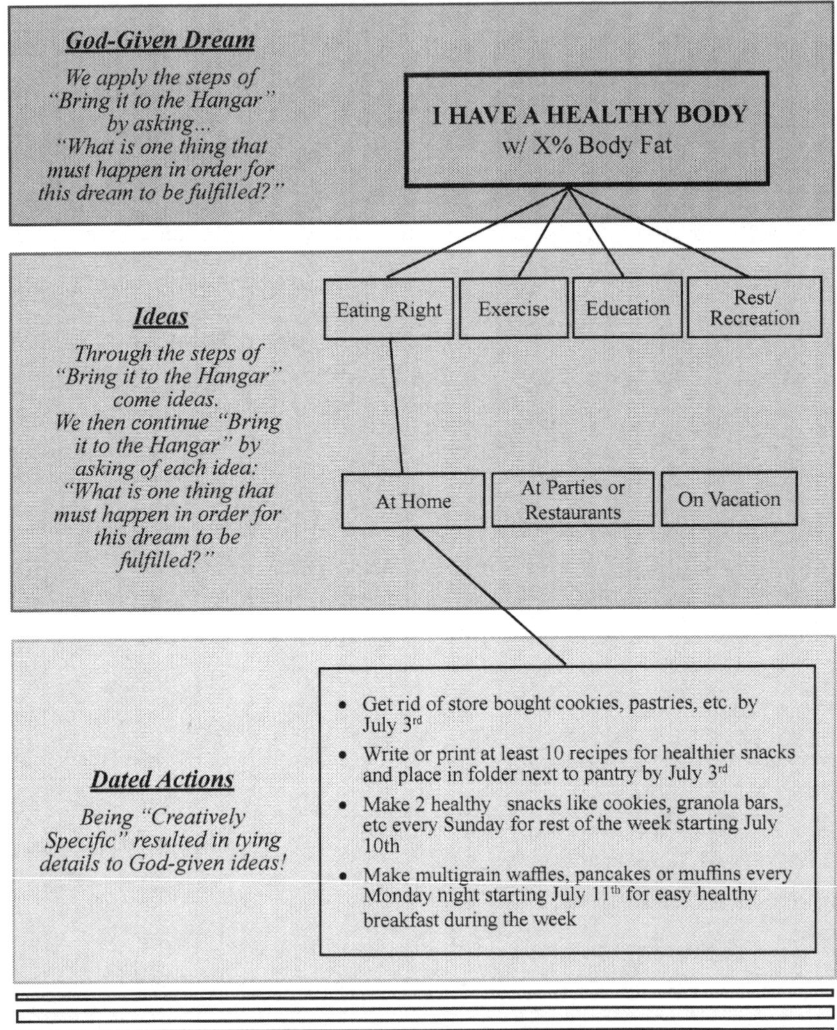

Dated Actions bring our God-given dream "*...to the Hangar!*" by forcing us to productivity. Once at this level, our God-given dream has nowhere to go but up. If we find that our actions seem vague, we should continue to ask ourselves these same questions until our plane is grounded in *Dated Actions*.

Everyone needs to be a "pen-to-paper *Dated Actions* maker" whether they are a visual person or not. In FORWARD THINKING, I spent time talking about the importance of writing out our dream so we can reinforce it by seeing it and reading it often.[5] Our *Dated Actions* should be a mini daily or weekly version of our God-given dream.

So, where should we place these *Dated Actions*? Later, as we develop the *Means* of GENERATE A PLAN and HAVE ACCOUNTABILITY, we will land the plane regarding tools that can help us do just that. But, for now, my *Creatively Specific* answer is that we should put *Dated Actions* where we will see them the most. The most effective *Dated Actions* are mobile ones. Carrying our *Dated Actions* with us either in an electronic or pen-to-paper calendar helps make them easily accessible and usable.

When we bring our God-given dream "... *to the Hangar!*" we become a person of action. As we land the plane, we will then be able to prepare for the next phase of LINK ACTIONS TO IDEAS. By being *Creatively Specific* in our landing, we are now ready to apply that same process as we begin to "*Takeoff!*"

Gate #4 - CONNECTOR QUESTION
Why do it (whatever the action is)?

Maneuver: *"Takeoff!"*

The first question in LINK ACTIONS TO IDEAS is about the specifics; the next question focuses more on the "Why?" behind it. Just like being *Creatively Specific* helps us *"Bring it to the Hangar!"* a similar approach must be taken in the opposite direction when it comes to ideas.

Maintenance: Link, Speak, Pray

When we apply the *"Bring it to the Hangar!"* steps, we Pray, Speak, and Link. By asking questions we Link ideas to *Dated Actions*. When we *"Takeoff!"* we simply ask, "Why?" When we ask "Why?" we Link that action upwards. As we Speak these answers, we are then led to the idea and ultimately back to Pray over our God-given dream.

As an example of the previous diagram, we would ask…

- "Why do I need to get rid of all of the store-bought cookies, cakes, pastries, etc. by July 3rd?" (Refer to the previous "Bring it to the Hangar!" visual layout.) The answer should be something in the vicinity of: "to eliminate temptation in my house" or "to save money in order to spend on purchasing healthier alternatives" or the like.

- Then, we would ask another "Why?" question. The answer should be something like: "So that my goal of eating healthier is supported within my home."

- We keep going up by asking (you guessed it) "Why?" And the answer should point directly to the dream God gave us of "Having a Healthy Body with X% Body Fat." The "Why?" question links our actions back to the ideas that link to our God-given dream.

All this asking "Why?" lends itself to ask "Why ask, why?" This process of asking "Why?" will help us "know that we know" - thereby gaining understanding that motivates us to take action.

Every actual flight uses a safety check. "*Takeoff!"* is the safety check to LINK ACTIONS TO IDEAS.

The first few times that I taught "*Bring it to the Hangar!"* to managers in planning and goal setting classes I did not teach the process of "*Takeoff!"* By the third or so class, I realized that once managers returned to their territories only a small percentage were applying their action steps. It was not that "*Bring it to the Hangar!"* was not helping. Without the "Why?" step many managers let go of their motivation because their actions did not link to anything personal. Answering the "Why?" question makes it personal. When it is personal, it is linked to something more than ideas or actions. The truth is that God gives us dreams filled with ideas, so it is already personal to God.

The answers to these "Why?" questions ultimately lead us to our purpose that will give the *Means* of FLIGHT focus. Why we do something is what motivates us to do it. Writing down ideas and *Dated Actions* is very important because it gives us something tangible to track. Without the "Why?" questions being answered, even tangible ideas and actions can be easily put aside.The interesting thing is that (once we begin asking the "Why?" question) we may quickly move past the idea straight to the God-given dream. For some, they will know "Why?" God gave them a certain dream at the time they received the dream; for most, they will need to discover the "Why?" along the way.

Applying "*Takeoff!*" helps us discover the "Why?" behind our God-given dream. As we take our God-given dream to FLIGHT, "*Takeoff!*" enables us to Link the action as we Speak (by asking "Why?") and reveal to us what we should Pray. Many times when I have applied "*Takeoff!*" it stretched me to remember a Scripture that gave lift to the dream God gave me.

However, back to our example from earlier, considering that "*Bring it to the Hangar!*" helps us land the plane, "*Takeoff!*" gets the *Means* of FLIGHT up in the air. The following is a visual application of "*Takeoff!*"

"Take Off"

Remember, you are moving up when you "Take Off!"

(Link, Speak, Pray)

This visual reads from bottom to top.

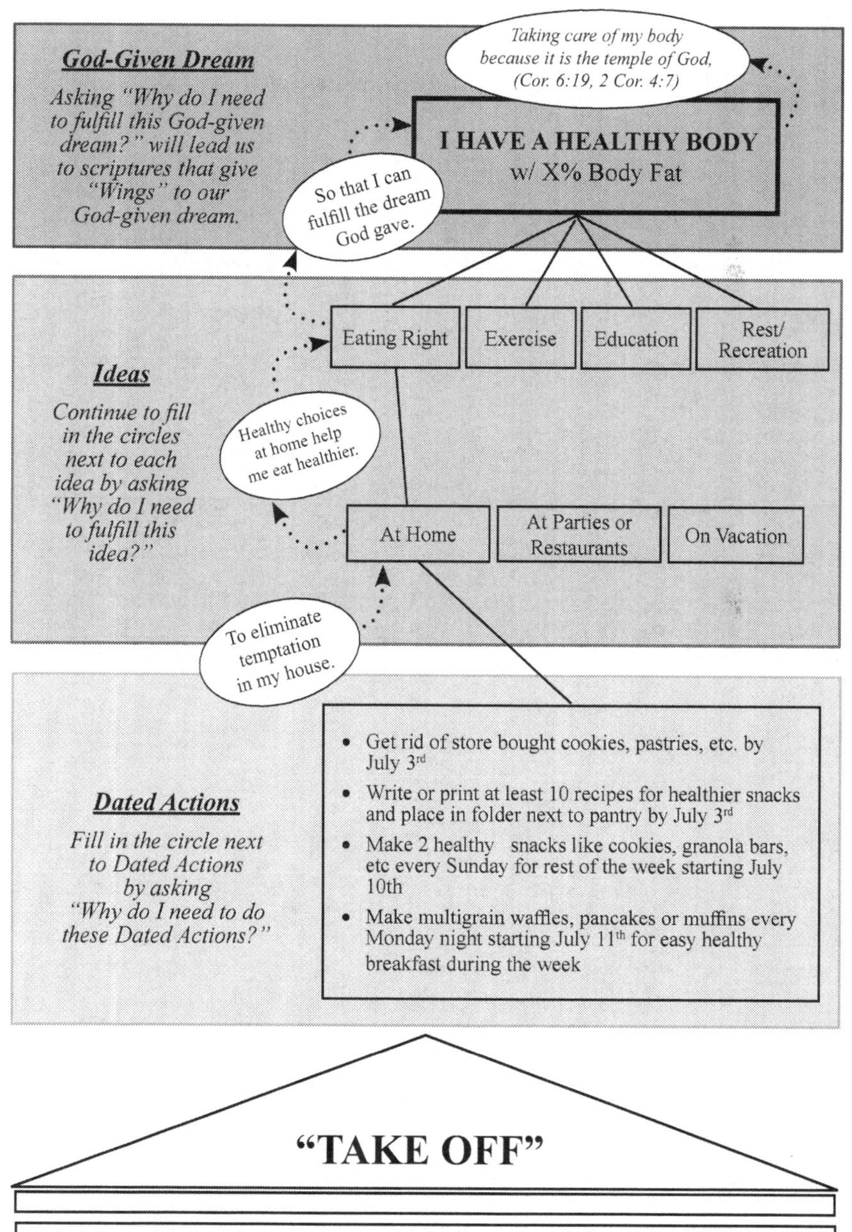

"TAKE OFF"

As you can see, "*Takeoff!*" is more than the reverse of "*Bring it to the Hangar!*" "*Takeoff!*" is what gives *lift* to the *Means* of FLIGHT by helping us **persevere**. When we "*Takeoff!*" with *Dated Actions*, ideas, and our God-given dream, the *Means* of FLIGHT ascends to new heights.

"*Bring it to the Hangar!*" and "*Takeoff!*" LINK ACTIONS TO IDEAS helping us set and fulfill goals. Once we have ideas linked to actions and then link actions back to those ideas, we know what we need to do as well as why we need to do it. This knowledge helps us create goals. Goals are simply written ideas linked to *Dated Actions* and a dream.

During that flight years ago when God placed these metaphors on my heart, I remember the anticipation, excitement, energy, and encouragement as the plane lifted into the sky. I believe that is the same experience we should have as we apply "*Takeoff!*" in FLIGHT.

Just like with Jacob, when we seek God first, He will give us the most *Creatively Specific* ideas and actions to move the dream that He has given us forward. When we can embrace LINK ACTIONS TO IDEAS, we will develop the skill of being *Creatively Specific* and solidify the dream in our hearts.

Let's review as we "*Now finish the work!*" In LINK ACTION TO IDEAS, we have passed through two very important gates by asking two very important questions.

Along with their Maneuvers and Maintenance, these questions will help us develop the *Means* to fulfill our God-given dreams.

LINK ACTIONS TO IDEAS

Gate #3 - CONNECTOR QUESTION
How do I land this plane *Creatively Specific*?

Maneuver: "*Bring it to the Hangar!*"
Maintenance: Pray, Speak, Link

Gate #4 - CONNECTOR QUESTION
Why do it (whatever the action is)?

Maneuver: "*Takeoff!*"
Maintenance: Link, Speak, Pray

Whether our dream is to restructure the way we do our family finances or rebuild an old car for competition, LINK ACTIONS TO IDEAS helps us "*Bring it to the Hangar!*" and "*Takeoff!*" These landings and takeoffs keep our dreams moving forward.

Momentum helps us hold on to **passion** and **perseverance** so that we are not merely excited out of the gate but determined to get to where God knows that we can be. At this point, we are then prepared to fly out of an area called ***A Time to Create*** and into the middle air space of ***A Time to Generate.*** In ***A Time to Generate***, we can develop the *Means* of INVOLVE THOSE NEEDED.

Before we move on to our next *Means* of FLIGHT, however, it is important to do an In-FLIGHT Check that will help us get to where God knows that we can be. This application is sure to ignite **passion** and **perseverance** that will help us…

Develop *Means* by Connecting *Wings* to God-Given Dreams

On the following page is a merged diagram of *"Bring it to the Hangar!"* and *"Takeoff!"* By filling in this graphic we make the *Means* of LINK ACTIONS TO IDEAS personal.

"Bring it to the Hangar" (Pray, Speak, Link)

1. Write your God-given dream in the top rectangle box.
2. Fill in the flow chart by applying the *"Bring it to the Hangar!"* steps.
3. As you go down, remember to ask the following question: "What is one thing that must happen to fulfill this dream or idea?"
4. Fill in each rectangle, asking this same question; Remember: *Think Creatively Specific* tying details to God-given ideas.

"Takeoff!" - Going back up the page - (Link, Speak, Pray)

5. Ask the "Why?" questions to be able to fill in the ovals. (see *"Takeoff!"* section) The top oval should be Scriptures of **passion** and **perseverance** that will connect *Wings* to the particular God-given dream you are developing.

As we develop the *Means* of LINK ACTIONS TO IDEAS, we prepare to travel to a place where His plans can be generated.

In-FLIGHT Check

Recording what we learn along the way will help us develop beyond today!

"Link Actions to Ideas"

"BRING IT TO THE HANGAR" Fill in boxes from top to bottom.
"TAKE OFF" Fill in circles from bottom to top.

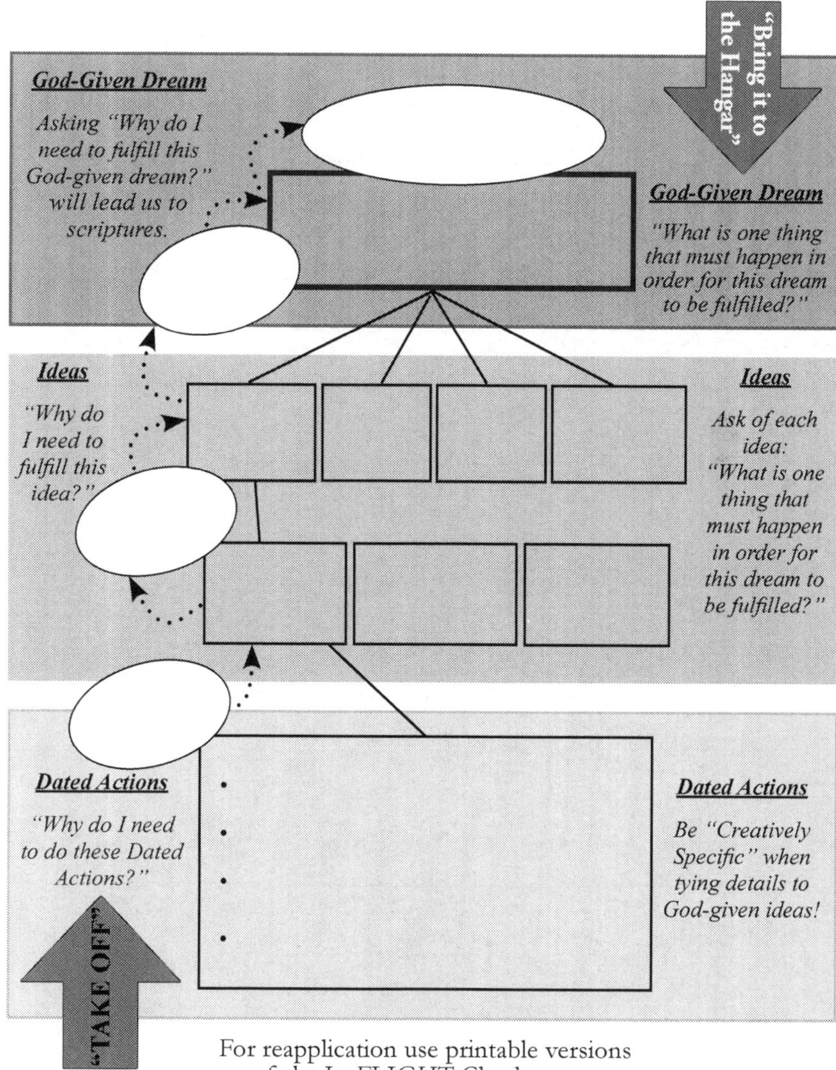

For reapplication use printable versions of the In-FLIGHT Check pages, go to the link below to access these and other resources:

www.yourflightplans.com/tools

A Time To Generate

Generate: to bring into existence, to originate by a vital, chemical, or physical process[1]

A Time to Generate is the difference maker between a person with a dream and a person realizing that dream. We can bring into existence or generate by actively developing the *Means* of INVOLVE THOSE NEEDED, GENERATE A PLAN, and HAVE ACCOUNTABILITY.

As we fly into this middle airspace, God will lead us to the right **people**, giving us revelation through **planning** as He encourages, corrects, and directs us to the highest levels of **productivity**. ***A Time to Generate*** is when our God-given dreams become reality: where our actions meet accomplishment.

Chapter Three

INVOLVE THOSE NEEDED

Years ago, I experienced the importance of air communication while flying shotgun in a two-seater airplane. When I was in my early twenties, I traveled to the State of Kansas to visit my sister and her in-laws over Christmas vacation. While I was there, my sister's brother-in-law, a pilot, offered to take us for an amazing Christmas light tour of the city. Now, I had lived in or near this Kansas town for ten years of my life growing up. Although I was used to frigid, snowy, winter nights, I had never flown in such nights - let alone in a small airplane taking off on a very icy runway. Regardless, I pressed through. When it was my turn, I climbed into the cockpit, buckled up, and put on my gear (all while sporting an anxious smile).

When flying in a small aircraft in the depth of winter, I learned that long underwear and thick outerwear are your best friends. There were no blue blankets or complimentary coffee. Once on the runway, I briefly took off my earphones to adjust my toboggan. Loud does not even begin to describe the sound that rang through my head. It is amazing how much noise those little earphones blocked.

Immediately, I began to notice the importance of having the right people involved in taking this plane to flight. Before we took off, the pilot explained to me how he had to account for my extra weight. Not taking offense I listened as he told me that it was not a personal dig but rather basic physics. A small plane flies differently with an extra person on board. From the beginning of our flight, I was more than just a passenger. I had become a co-pilot - helping to adjust things needed in the small allotted space for the comfort of us both. On the runway, I listened as my pilot talked with air traffic control and watched him check off a list with much detail and concentration. Although he had flown many times before, he explained to me that this routine was a safety check and a must before any flight. It seemed as though he not only knew what he was doing but who else to involve when needed.

Then, it was time to take off. With confidence, the pilot maneuvered the plane down the runway. I could feel every bump and icy patch as our two wheels sped between the lines and lifted us off the ground. Once in the air, we buzzed through the night sky and tilted our way towards a cruising altitude. The successful takeoff was behind us.

Although it was even colder in the air than it had been on the ground, I hardly noticed, for I was enthralled with the view before and below me. The pilot was continually pointing out the spectacular scenery along the way. Looking out my window, I was mesmerized by what I saw. For miles, thousands of lights sparkled on the snow-covered, flat Kansas terrain. It was breathtaking!

As I enjoyed the view, I remember listening to the pilot tell me how safe flying was because of the communication and teamwork between the pilots and the airport. This confident pilot explained to me that, although it seemed as if we were alone in the sky, someone always knew our coordinates, gauge readings, and expected time of arrival.

Finally, when we came in for a landing, it became clearer that we were not a solo flight. In the frigid air, we quickly deplaned and headed into the small, but very warm, lobby. Once inside, we were greeted with a friendly smile and a genuine, "So, how was the flight?" from the receptionist and airport manager who were both working behind the counter. All of us, myself included, shared in this unique experience of getting a small plane up into the air and safely back into its hangar. For the success of our small flight, it took a group of people - the right people - to get us to our destination.

Over the years, that flight experience has helped me gain perspective about the importance of the *Means* of INVOLVE THOSE NEEDED. Knowing "who" to involve helps our God-given dream take FLIGHT. Whether our God-given dream seems as big as a 747 or as small as a twin prop plane, INVOLVE THOSE NEEDED can be the difference between "how" or "if" we arrive at the destination that God has planned for us.

While FORWARD THINKING and LINK ACTIONS TO IDEAS give us *Wings* of **passion** and **perseverance**, we must remember that we are not the only ones that are impacted by what we do. God never intends our journey to be a solo one. No matter how big or small an aircraft may be when taking FLIGHT, it requires multiple **people** for the journey to be a success.

People are not perfect. Our FLIGHT will experience some turbulence as we work with others; but, along with the bumps are some great advantages. Memories, laughter, camaraderie, and support are many by-products of a great team relationship. Building a great team, however, does not happen by accident - it happens on purpose.

I have a lot to learn about bringing a team together, but I have been blessed to learn from some of the best team builders. In the mid-1990s, I worked for a restaurant company that planned an aggressive worldwide expansion of their business. Because there were only a few of us who committed to continual travel and living out of suitcases from city to city, our small group quickly became versed in the ins and outs of opening their new sites. Over time, seven of us divided up the globe and partnered with franchise owners and executives to lead and train teams to accomplish the company's vision. I worked alongside many executives - taking notice of how to lead teams to accomplish a specific goal successfully. This knowledge became invaluable as I developed and led my teams.

Coming up through the ranks (working on different teams in many different cultures, cities, and under different ownerships), I began to see a pattern of success and failure. I came to recognize that - without people, the God-given dream we take to FLIGHT cannot sustain the trip, and minus good communication, our trip cannot sustain the people.

INVOLVE THOSE NEEDED - through good communication - helped me establish multiple leaders to head up teams of experienced and passionate trainers throughout my career. Because of pride, however, I limited myself in how to apply what I had learned to other areas of my life. It was not until I left the workforce that I realized how INVOLVE THOSE NEEDED is the heartbeat of God Himself.

It makes sense, for this reason, to begin INVOLVE THOSE NEEDED by first seeking the Word of God concerning communication.

Gate #5 - CONNECTOR QUESTION
What did "Air Traffic Control" say today?

Maneuver: Concordance and Coordinates

Knowing where we are today will help us find our way. Once our eyes are open to where we are in our development, we are then able to see our next steps more clearly. Regarding others, if we do not know where we are in our development:

- We do not know who should jump aboard.
- We cannot give direction to those that join us.
- We face difficulty being led towards someone who could help.
- We become unattractive to others, as people are not attracted to people who fly in circles.

The first one that we should seek is "The One" who gave us the dream in the first place. The surest way to find out where we are is to seek God.[1] Our Father God - our "Air Traffic Control" - will use concordance (agreement through His Word) to give us our coordinates (where we are and where we could go). When we spend time with God, He will often direct us back to His Word. The Word teaches us "right where we are" so that we can get to "where He knows that we can be."

When we go to God first, He will show us whom to glean guidance from and how and when to apply it. Of course, to "*Now finish the work!*" and develop the *Means* of INVOLVE THOSE NEEDED, there is some Maintenance involved. So in keeping with the Cs of concordance and coordinates, let's develop three more Cs.

Maintenance: Call, Consider, Carry

Call

The first chapter of FLIGHT is devoted to discovering a God-given dream or a "call" that God puts in our hearts. Sometimes, we can become so focused on a "big" dream that we miss the dream God has for us right now. When I stopped waiting for "the" call on my life and started answering His daily calls, I began to discover God's plan for my life. The biggest revelation of this discovery was that His plans for me, and for all of us, are based on us connecting with others. In other words, God wants us to develop the *Means* of INVOLVE THOSE NEEDED.

When I think about the word "call" (as a verb), I immediately go to ***Jeremiah 29:12***. This verse helps me to see specific communication in a different and powerful way.

"Then you will call upon Me and go and pray to Me, and I will listen to you."
(Jer. 29:12 NKJV)

This verse is about how we learn the plans God has for us. God also showed me this verse as a template for developing the *Means* of INVOLVE THOSE NEEDED. When we call upon someone, it is an active display of communication. It takes initiative to pick up a phone or reach out to someone. These small acts demonstrate that we care about the other person. Whether we are interviewing someone for a position with our company or reaching out to check a person's interest in a project, our call is usually the next step after God places this person on our heart.

Now, there are times when God may just show us a glimpse of how this person will be involved in the dream that He has given us. If God gives us the "go ahead" to connect with a person - and we wait, then our hesitation could hinder the journey to both our and that person's destination.

Once a call has been made, the next step is to prioritize spending time with this person. Face-to-face meetings build relationships by eliminating distance. I remember one time in particular that I had taken over a territory in the Manhattan area of New York. I traveled to the area with my boss to be introduced to the franchise owners and many of their employees. Because they had never had a consultant to help them, that face-to-face meeting set the pace for a vibrant relationship that restored trust in their parent company and established more open communication. This relationship helped me to develop influence in their business practices. Eventually, this led to a thriving partnership that transformed one of their training stores into an example store for not only their market but for markets in other countries. There is something about being around other people that breaks down barriers and helps develop new opportunities.

The right communication between people should be modeled after the right communication with God. Prayer is the ultimate "bringer together" of distance. Prayer is designed not only as a means for us to listen and speak with God but is also a template of how to communicate with one another. There have been many times I have prayed and talked way more than listened, and I have fallen into that same scenario with people. Good communication has both components (talking and listening); but, as individuals, we may need to develop in one or both of these areas.

It is true that people do not care how much a person knows until they know how much that person cares. Listening (actively hearing what someone is saying) helps us to develop compassion that opens the door to our having influence in the other person's life. We should all take the time to think about how we pray and to ask ourselves, who does most of the talking?

When we reach out to those to whom God has connected us, we must be willing to listen to their needs, wants, and desires. We can glean much knowledge of how to help someone or to determine if we are a good match for partnership with someone simply by keeping quiet and listening to what is coming out of someone's mouth.

Less than a year before I was promoted to be a traveling supervisor/consultant for that restaurant company, I received a lesson in listening. I was asked to open a new location with fewer people than were normally allocated to help me implement training. I was also given a new trainer. I had met this particular trainer during his interview stage and had recommended that he not be assigned to this position as he was not ready for the role that he was seeking. Not only was I concerned about his skills but also his ability to work in high-pressure situations. He was hired by his market, yet I was assigned to develop his skills (since I brought his deficiencies to their attention). The skill of "active listening" would prove to help me in this challenging situation.

During the first week on-site, I had multiple conversations with this individual about taking initiative and (you guessed it) following through on his responsibilities as a trainer helping to open a multi-million dollar establishment within two weeks. I emphasized that every second of productivity meant money earned or lost. While continually directing him back to his contractual agreement, I encouraged him that his behavior could change simply by adhering to what he said that he could do when he signed on for his new role. Then it happened. During one of his shifts - he snapped; although not literally, he did speak harshly at one of our client's employees. I then escorted him into a private meeting. Although I had a lot that I wanted to say, I knew that applying "active listening" would help me lead us through this difficult situation. I asked questions and let him talk. This young man eventually revealed (to himself and me) that he had broken his contract. By listening more than speaking, I was able to discern the truth that gave me a better sense of how to handle the situation.

It is in the "call" that we begin the process of developing the *Means* of INVOLVE THOSE NEEDED. By understanding that God has called all of us into a relationship with Him and His people, we can then actively pursue those people in our lives that can help us take our dream to FLIGHT. As ***Jeremiah 29:12*** states, God will listen when we properly communicate. So will God's people when we properly communicate with them. The verse right after this tells us that, when we seek God with all of our heart, we will find Him. As we develop a heart for God - that is people - developing the *Means* of INVOLVE THOSE NEEDED will become easier.

Consider

Reaching out to those people that God has connected our God-given dream to is very important. Equally as important is to consider where those people fit into our team. Leading a team (whether to coordinate an overnight retreat or manage a yearly fundraiser) means having people in the correct positions. It is so important to involve God in every aspect of our journey; this area is no different.

Before we INVOLVE THOSE NEEDED, it is vital that we consider. "Consider what?" you might ask. In ***Proverbs 6:6-8***, God tells us to "consider" the ways of the ant. God then describes what the ant does to fulfill its role as an ant. In fact, each ant has a different role within its colony. When each ant fulfills its assigned role, the ants operate as a unified entity, collectively working together to support the colony and complete the work that God has for them.

A leader should want not only his/her dream to succeed, but the people to succeed who help with that dream. Setting people up for success will help our dreams reach their destinations. When we consider the role of those involved, we will become a better leader and will help develop other leaders.

While writing this book, I conducted a meeting with some leaders who were discussing how they would structure a new business venture and specifically who to involve. I took these leaders through some FLIGHT principles. A few weeks after that meeting, God gave me an acrostic that can help leaders consider how to develop the *Means* of INVOLVE THOSE NEEDED.

STOW

Strengths

Time

Opportunities

Weaknesses

In FLIGHT phraseology, to go, we must STOW when considering a team. One area in which I loved to teach when I was training managers was the area of staffing and retention. Having someone join a team is one thing, but keeping them around involves a whole different level of leadership. While conducting exit interviews for a company, I learned that - people leave people - not companies, businesses, or organizations. Taking the time to consider people on the front end is a worthwhile investment for everyone involved.

People are the core of God's heart. As stated before, if we want to fulfill the plans God has for our lives, we must put people at the core of our heart, too. Doing so does not mean that when we INVOLVE THOSE NEEDED that everyone we come in contact with or know should be a part of the team to help take our dreams to FLIGHT. The "needed" part of INVOLVE THOSE NEEDED is because certain people are needed for certain dreams while others are needed to help fulfill someone else's dream. So, how do we know if someone is a great fit to help with our God-given dream? STOW can help us.

Strengths: When we consider someone, we must assess that person's **strengths** in relationship to taking our God-given dream to FLIGHT. A person may be a genius physician, but we may need someone with stellar auto mechanic skills; for this reason, that physician would not be a good fit. Or, what if we already had three very analytical people on our team, then we might want to consider bringing on someone who is more artistically creative. We should consider how this person would work alongside the other people on the team. Skills are important, but so is team dynamic. When we first consider what strengths we need to help us reach our destinations - whether in skill or personality - we will better recognize when people with those strengths come into our lives.

When putting together teams, I learned to consider the dynamic of the company culture along with the strengths of each person on that team. Some of my team members worked better with certain people rather than others. I remember, one time one of my peers was putting together a team to help open a new site in another country. He came to me to help him build a team that would work well together in that environment. Although many individuals had strengths in ability and attitude, only a few also had the flexibility to work in certain conditions. It was not that the other people were not quality leaders; it was that they simply did not qualify for that specific destination.

We took time putting together a team of leaders (and even scheduled some supervisors, including myself) in trainer positions. During that trip, our team encountered first-time experiences and challenges that required very delicate communication. These skills far exceeded normal company best practice knowledge. When putting together effective teams, it should not be about titles but rather strengths that help develop the *Means* of FLIGHT for that particular destination.

Time: **An** important factor is **time** when we INVOLVE THOSE NEEDED. I have learned that priorities tell us a lot about how people value their time. Whether people are paid, and especially when they are not paid, time valued per individual is critical to helping one develop a team.

Understanding how someone values time, takes more time than an interview will allow. But, when we need to hire someone who we have never worked with, there are certain questions that can help us consider whether this person is the right person. Open-ended questions require more than a simple "yes" or "no" answer. These questions help to paint a picture of a particular time when someone has or has not valued time. For example, questions like:

- "Describe a time when you helped your boss or a coworker with his/her time?" This question will paint a picture of a person's history, as well as reveal how this person defines helping someone with his/her time.

- "Explain a time when you worked, led, or helped with a project? Specifically, what was your role, how did you manage your time, and how did your time affect those also involved?" This question can help the interviewer better understand the process of how this person manages their time, as well as how their time impacts another person's time.

- "What does 'on time' mean to you?" This question enables the person to explain how they value time. It will also give the interviewer the opportunity to state company parameters on this very important expectation.

Opportunities and **W**eaknesses: When it comes to opportunities and weaknesses I have heard many people say that these two areas are much more challenging to discern, however, in the right environment they are not. After my career in business I began home schooling our children. As the years went by God put a dream in some of my friends' hearts to start a tutorial school for middle through high school students. Because of my strengths in organization they asked me to help them launch it. I shared with them about my strengths and my time. I was also very candid with them regarding my **opportunities**, areas that I was confident that I could develop in, and my **weaknesses**, those areas which I knew that I should not waste their time or mine trying to improve. Later, when we began interviewing teachers our interviewing panel used personal examples of our own opportunities and weaknesses. During these interviews teachers frequently told us their areas of opportunities and weaknesses. Creating an environment where people feel safe to share about themselves, not only encourages integrity, but allows opportunities and weakness to be dealt with effectively.

It is important to note that even when we consider people, they may not always be completely honest with us or we may make a mistake; but, we still must keep moving forward. There have been many times that I have promoted or "laterally moved" people into what I thought would be the best fit for everyone only to find out that I was one-hundred percent wrong. Granted, this happened more often the less I sought God during this process.

None of us are perfect; we will make mistakes along the way. But, when we involve God, the gap between our mistakes and the time it takes to fix them will shrink to a place that yields much more productivity.

When we do what is right (regardless of whether it puts us in a bind initially), eventually it will reap better results. Referring to my story of the trainer, I gave him choices, none of which he wanted to take. By not choosing any of the options laid before him, he inadvertently chose to lose his position on my team. Even though I was already working with a skeleton crew, I still had to make the right decision to protect my team and the company's investment.

Once the dust settled, I called a team meeting and explained (without too many details) the situation we were facing. With my and my team's jobs on the line (regardless of doing the right thing), I had to deliver to our clients a trained management team and staff that produced financial results. I encouraged the team that we would rather have a smaller, stronger, and united team than one with a weakness that could cause delays. Such delays could ultimately hurt our relationship with the region in which we received our contractual work. I was honest with my team and explained that the workload would increase. I encouraged them that if we worked together as a team servicing the needs of our partners, a "job well done" would open doors for us to consult in more lucrative locations. The team was motivated. We worked together to finish our assignment in the face of adversity, working very long shifts for multiple days back-to-back.

The result was a loyal and successful team. That team went on to travel all over the United States with me, and everyone was promoted into leadership positions. With so *many* locations requesting our team, I was able to promote some of these loyal people to go in my place as I supervised from a distance. Each one of those team members became loyal to me and, more importantly, to the vision. I believe this loyalty was because I rightfully honored the agreement we all signed, even when it meant losing manpower.

Looking back, I had followed STOW when I interviewed each of those leaders:

- By determining if their **strengths** matched the team that was needed to fulfill the vision,
- By confirming that they were willing to put the **time** into the position,
- By explaining a realistic vision of the **opportunities** that would come with the work that they put forth, and
- By assessing their **weaknesses** to help them develop and grow as a member of the team.

STOW helped me consider how to INVOLVE THOSE NEEDED; and, ultimately, by applying STOW, we all benefited. Through adversity, we succeeded. We STOWed up our **strengths** (by delegating to whom could get the job done the best). We STOWed up our **time** (by working extra hard on that site). We STOWed up our **opportunities** (because of our persistence and hard work). And, we STOWed up our **weaknesses** (by cutting our losses even when it was the hard thing to do).

Carry

"I thank my God every time I remember you. In all my prayers for all of you, I always pray with joy because of your partnership in the gospel from the first day until now, being confident of this, that he who began a good work in you will carry it on to completion until the day of Christ Jesus."
(Phil. 1:3-6 NIV)

Carrying too much of anything can overload even the most developed *Means* of FLIGHT. We must be able to distribute effectively for our God-given dream to *Takeoff!*

Years ago, while boarding an express commuter plane (along with maybe ten other passengers), I received a lesson in distribution. Before takeoff, a flight attendant came into the main area and, with a cheery disposition, asked us kindly to reposition. It was like the "guess my weight" game at the county fair as we were sized up and shifted down or up the aisle. Luggage moved from overhead to overhead as all shapes and sizes moved forward, backward, and side-to-side. Finally, we were able to distribute our weight to the exceptional level of counterbalance. We all buckled up in our new locations and prepared for takeoff.

Aside from playing musical chairs, I also remember the flight attendant's words to a not-so-compliant passenger. The flight attendant said something along the lines of: "If we do not distribute the weight on this plane, none of us will be going anywhere." These words are a powerful truth, not only on a plane, but also when developing the *Means* of INVOLVE THOSE NEEDED.

So, what exactly does the term "carry" mean in reference to developing the *Means* of INVOLVE THOSE NEEDED? While "carry" does imply delegation and follow-through on performance, it goes beyond simply getting something done. In the business world, I learned "call" through good communication and "consider" through the art of the interview and retention. However, it was not until God showed me the true definition of "successful distribution" that I was able to "carry" a God-given dream. This revelation came through one word found in ***Philippians 1:5*** - partnership!

The journey we take to fulfill our God-given dream
is not a solo trip but a partnership.

The term partnership is often looked at from a status point of view, but it is much more than that. We better understand the full meaning of partnership when we consider that the Apostle Paul associated it with our ability to complete the work. There is nowhere (that I know of) in the book of Philippians that Paul mentions titles in reference to these partners. For years, I worked, as do many while climbing the corporate ladder, to receive a new and more prestigious title. Obtaining such a status seemed the pinnacle of success. Those who worked for me also jockeyed for a position; and, although I did my best to foster an environment of healthy competition, there was always a title dictating a behavior simply for the sake of recognition.

As I studied God's Word, I began to understand what a difference a true partnership makes - especially as we relate it to the FLIGHT term "carry." When we work in an environment with the mindset that we are working to obtain a title, we will never be fulfilled - there will always be another title just beyond our reach. It is when we work with others - with God - that we realize that we have already made "partner" because God is now partnering with us. This revelation changed my whole life. Many people will be called and considered; few will become a partner.

In applying STOW, those people whose reliability in their responsibility gives us an indication of who could begin to carry some weight. We can more easily "*Now finish the work!*"

when those helping to carry the dream fulfill the description of the word itself.

Carry: to move while supporting[3]

This definition of "carry" is a powerful description of what someone in "partnership" should be doing. As I type this, I am both convicted and encouraged to develop my role as a partner. What an awesome job description to *"Now finish the work!"* while supporting the person pursuing his/her God-given dream. What responsibility, but what an honor!

People, just like those who helped a little two-seater airplane land during a snowy December night, are vital to taking a God-given dream to FLIGHT. INVOLVE THOSE NEEDED is important to God; so, it should be important to us as well. God is the "Master Communicator." He will connect our lives with people that are willing to go the distance if we listen to His call, consider how we can STOW to Go, and pursue those partners who will commit to carrying the dream. He will then take us to a place where He can help us to GENERATE A PLAN that gives us and others hope and a future.

So, let's review. In INVOLVE THOSE NEEDED, we have passed through one very important gate by asking one very important question. This question, along with its Maneuver and Maintenance, will help us develop the *Means* to fulfill our God-given dream.

INVOLVE THOSE NEEDED

Gate #5 - CONNECTOR QUESTION
What did "Air Traffic Control" say today?

Maneuver: Concordance and Coordinates
Maintenance: Call, Consider, Carry

We have begun to develop the *Means* of INVOLVE THOSE NEEDED by partnering with God and the right **people**. It is time to "*Now finish the work!*" as we jot down some things that we have learned by asking this important gate question. This In-FLIGHT Check will help us get to where God knows that we can be. It is true that with the right **people,** we...

Develop *Means* by Connecting *Wings* to God-Given Dreams

In-FLIGHT Check

Recording what we learn along the way will help us develop beyond today!

Develop *Means* of INVOLVE THOSE NEEDED by answering this Connector Question: "What did 'Air Traffic Control' say today?"

Call:

____

____

____

____

Consider (STOW to Go):

____

____

____

____

Carry:

____

____

____

____

Connecting *Wings* of **people**: Seek God and write out Scriptures that lift the answer to the above question.

____

____

____

____

____

____

____

____

Now it is time to GENERATE A PLAN!

For reapplication use printable versions
of the In-FLIGHT Check pages,
go to the link below to access these and other resources:

www.yourflightplans.com/tools

Chapter Four

GENERATE A PLAN

Niagara Falls (a dream vacation for many honeymooners) was the destination written on the email assignment in my inbox. I had taken a few days off; the night before I returned to work, I opened my email and found a red-flagged message from my boss.

I began to get excited as I read and comprehended the email's message that I would be traveling to Canada on a month-long business trip. I anticipated that, in addition to working long hours, I might be able to enjoy at least an afternoon gazing at the world-renowned waterfalls. I began to embrace the opportunity that I was blessed to be chosen to help the company I worked for launch into a new international market. The language was not an issue and, for the most part, the culture was similar to many of the New England locations I had worked in over the years. The trip was sure to bring some challenges, but I knew that I was prepared to help build relationships with our friends across the United States' border.

Based on the information in the letter, I would need to leave in a few months - which would have given me plenty of time to cover my responsibilities in the states. In a matter of minutes, I had convinced myself that this was going to be a great trip.

And then - I got the call that changed everything. "What do you think about spending a month or so in Cairo, Egypt, instead of Canada? I need your help with this one. They specifically requested you. This assignment may link up with some other international assignments making it a longer trip. And oh, by the way, you will need to leave in a few weeks."

As I listened and began to process my boss' voicemail message, images of me being sprayed by the mist of an enormous waterfall faded from my mind. Quickly, looking at my calendar, I realized the magnitude of preparation work I would need to accomplish before departing to my new destination. Then there was the fact that I was trading in an August trip to the Great Lakes for thirty days plus in one of the hottest deserts in the world. Needless to say, it took more than a few minutes to sink in. This change in assignment would take more work than simply changing my flight from Canada to Cairo. I was looking at the beginning of a whole new plan.

What is a plan? Do not feel bad for wondering this because (as I was writing this book) I, too, revisited this same question. My favorite definition of a plan is as follows.

Plan: a method for achieving an end[1]

Defining a plan as a "method" is important as it helps to eliminate a cluttering effect that can bog us down when we are beginning to GENERATE A PLAN. A plan is not only a method, but it is a method that has an end. If it does not fit both of those criteria, it is simply a task and should *not* be overcomplicated. If we do not need a method - meaning if we do something so automatic that it does not need to be formulated - then *just do it, don't plan it!* I am sorry for yelling, but I needed to hear that even if you did not.

I have spoken to many people regarding **planning**, some who love planning and others who can't tell me enough about why they hate planning. There are many different personality types, some lending more to planning than others. People who think that they do not like to plan usually do so because, at some point, they have become overwhelmed by planning. A different response occurs from the plan-lovers. These individuals attempt to make everything a plan. Plan-lovers (although they may have beautiful lists, spreadsheets, and flipcharts) can become lost in the "method" of planning and never achieve the end.

Before we begin to develop the *Means* of GENERATE A PLAN, we should first make something very clear. These next words might disappoint some people or may arouse a round of applause from others. Either way, the words that we are about to read will change the way we approach planning. Read it twice. Read it aloud. Tell the person next to you. Write it down. Shout it from the rooftops.

I do not plan!

If you are quiet, you can hear the cheers of every non-planner on the planet at this very moment. Trying to plan is what gets in the way of fulfilling our God-given dreams. To many people, this does not even make sense because planning is how we get things done. Our plans help us complete our dreams, right? Yes, our plans help us complete our dreams. But, we must remember the difference between our being successful and being fulfilled. We can succeed or accomplish many things by planning; but, only when we develop *Means* by connecting *Wings* to God-given dreams are we fulfilled.

I realized I had a huge challenge ahead of me when my assignment changed from Canada to Cairo. I knew I had to have a plan. I immediately began to plan; but, in so doing, I missed the most important truth. I thought I needed to conceive and birth my plan: the truth is this God-conceived plan was ready for birth. All I needed to do was to bring the plan forward into my life. What I should have done was GENERATE A PLAN.

Generate: to bring into existence[2]

GENERATE A PLAN simply means to bring into existence a method to achieve an end. Our plans may be "in" us, but they should not be "of" us. As someone who plans, I have frequently found myself putting together my methods to achieve an end. Having had many opportunities to mess up a few plans, I have learned some things along the way. One of the most important things that I have learned about planning is how to GENERATE A PLAN. When we bring into existence the plan God has for us, we can then take our God-given dream to FLIGHT.

According to ***Jeremiah 29:11***, God has plans for both you and me. So, let's fasten our seatbelts, pull down our trays, and get out our papers and pens or electronic devices. Together, we can begin to develop the *Means* of GENERATE A PLAN.

Gate #6 - CONNECTOR QUESTION
"Why *GENERATE A PLAN*?"

Maneuver: *Wings* to God-given dreams

This question makes me smile. You see, for years, planning was all about me trying to hold myself accountable by formulating my checklists and agendas based on my timelines and experiences. Words, whether written or spoken, have significant power. By writing down goals, milestones, dates, to-do lists, agendas, spreadsheets, flip charts, PowerPoint presentations (you name it), I put together a work for my life.

Was this a successful approach? To be honest, it did bring much success. In my mid-twenties, I was promoted the youngest supervisor - overseeing store openings and the development of trainers - for a region spanning thirteen states for what later became one of the world's largest full-service restaurant companies. My career took off quickly, and the benefits were pleasing but not fulfilling. I had a knack for planning my way right into being a workaholic.

Even though I learned how to duplicate myself and my plans, I also developed an ongoing habit of not resting because

I always had a "plan of action for the next contraction." Just like in labor with a child, if a lady constantly contracts she will never relax enough to deliver. Constant planning is painful and very frustrating. But, thanks to God, His plans are for us to prosper - which is something that took me years to discover.

Generating a plan should be fulfilling, rewarding, and yes I will say it...FUN! For those of you who have never experienced such a thing, I encourage you to keep reading. I can honestly say that generating a plan is fun - not because I have a bent on planning but in spite of it! What I mean is that for years I successfully executed many plans, but I never found fulfillment through any of them. It was overwhelming yet exciting to change my travel Visa from Canada to Cairo, to reassign consultants for store openings and manage their complex travel schedules, and to do a quick study of the Arabic language and culture. Excited yes, but overwhelmed I should not have been because all I needed to do was GENERATE A PLAN. I simply should have brought forth the plan that God had already put together to prosper and not harm me.

So, why GENERATE A PLAN? God has a plan for us to prosper, and who does not want to prosper? If we are willing to bring into existence God's plan for us, instead of trying to make our plan, we will be on track to fulfill our God-given dream. We cannot take to FLIGHT without the "G." GENERATE A PLAN is smack dab in the middle of us taking to FLIGHT. Once we know "why" we should GENERATE A PLAN, we can move forward so we can develop "how" to do it.

Maintenance: Connect it, don't push it

I have discovered, through the Word of God, how to stop pushing a plan and instead connect it to *Wings* allowing God to give it lift. Usually pushing breaks a connection. The Word of God has the power to lift us out of any circumstance so long as we are willing to make a connection. This connection is what brings the development of "our" *Means* together with "God's" *Wings*. This connection is what will help us to fulfill our God-given dreams.

Pushing a God-given dream or any dream is when we try too hard in our strength by making our plans. When we push instead of connect, there will come a time when we cannot hold it together anymore. Without *Wings*, we cannot sustain any altitude that we have somehow been able to ascend to on our own.

You see, *Wings* take us to the place where lift occurs. *Wings* - the Word of God - connect our journey to the Holy Spirit. God's Spirit then lifts the *Means* of FLIGHT above all the storms, turbulence, and visual obstructions. Then, we will not only reach our destination, but we will be able to enjoy the journey in getting there.

Wings: the Word of God

When putting together a plan for building a plane, manufactured wings are a must. No matter how small or large an airplane appears to be, aircraft designers would not think twice about leaving out the wings in the blueprints of their designs. When we GENERATE A PLAN, God's Word must be included.

While it is true that some people are gifted planners, even the best planners - without the Word of God - will limit their potential if they do not connect to *Wings.*

Gate #7 - CONNECTOR QUESTION
"How do I *'Pre-Check'* the plan?"

Maneuver: The Pre-Check

Having traveled through the Connector Gates of LINK ACTIONS TO IDEAS, we have begun the process of connecting *Wings* to our God-given dreams. Learning to be *Creatively Specific* by applying "*Bring it to the Hangar!*" and "*Takeoff!*" to the ideas within our God-given dreams has set us up to GENERATE A PLAN. Our next step is to go through a Pre-Check before we begin the physical process of GENERATE A PLAN.

Maintenance: Emotional Check, God's Plans, and CHART the Details

Emotional Check

Before we can connect with our God-given dream, we must conduct an Emotional Check. When the going gets tough, will we side with our emotions or the generated plan? Emotions can get in the way of any God-given dream, but if we can check our emotions and focus on working the plan, then we can position ourselves for success.

Here is a visual regarding how to do an Emotional Check. When boarding a plane, the passengers must check their luggage at the gate, hand them over to a ground crew at the plane, or carry them on board. Regardless, each passenger's luggage must be secured in a safe place before takeoff. Similarly, we need to secure our emotions. We know we have them, but we must secure them; otherwise, at the first sign of turbulence, they will fall out and make things worse. Luggage, or our emotions, unchecked can cause our plans to change or even stop us from ever getting to our destination.

When we commit to working a plan, we, in turn, give no control to our emotions. Giving no control to our emotions does not make us emotionless - just less emotional. Controlling our emotions allows us to "*Now finish the work!*" The Wright Brothers did just that.

> In 1908 and 1909, Wilbur demonstrated Wright aircraft in Europe, and Orville flew in Fort Meyer, Virginia. The flights went well until Orville lost a propeller and crashed, breaking his leg and killing passenger Lt. Thomas Selfridge. While Orville recuperated, Wilbur kept flying in France, breaking record after record. Orville and his sister Kate eventually joined Wilbur in France, and the three returned home to Dayton, Ohio, to an elaborate homecoming celebration. Together, Orville and Wilbur returned to Fort Meyer with a new Military Flyer and completed the U.S. Army trials. A few months later, Wilbur flew before over

a million spectators in New York Harbor - his first public flight in his native land. All of these flights stunned and captivated the world. The Wright Brothers became the first great celebrities of the twentieth century.[3]

These two brothers met fierce opposition time and time again; such opposition can cause a person to succumb to their emotions. Imagine the emotional challenges Orville must have faced as he not only risked his life in pursuit of his God-given dream but also risked the life of another - that of passenger Lt. Selfridge. Then consider the anguish of having to face this person's family, as well as focus on his recovery, while his partner/brother/best friend was away in another country. Pressing past the emotions, Orville, once reunited with Wilbur, continued to strive to finish the work they had begun. They were able to stay focused on their plan - through the turbulence - because they first made a decision to check their emotions.

Throughout the history of aviation, we can find great men and women who checked their emotions as they kept moving towards their dream destinations.

- Raymonde DeLaroche was the first woman in the world to receive her pilot's license in 1910. She checked her emotions while receiving instruction. Raymonde was trained to fly by an instructor who remained on the ground as her plane only had room for one passenger.[4]

- The crew of the famous Memphis Belle, B-17 WWII Bomber, checked their emotions while under heavy attack completing their 25th mission to obtain ground status.[5]

- Operating on little to no sleep, Charles Lindbergh checked his emotions while facing naysayers and bad weather as he left a New York runway for his celebrated solo trip across the Atlantic Ocean. Against opposition, Charles chose to leave his radio behind, along with other items such as a parachute and gas gauges, to alleviate weight issues.[6]

These aviators and many more like them were able to finish a plan because they completed not only a flight check but an Emotional Check. Checking one's emotions will set up any plan for success. This discipline is a powerful force! I do not know if these pilots went beyond their means to GENERATE A PLAN. I do know, however, that if we do our part - by checking our emotions - we will be in a better position to ask God for help.

You might be thinking, "Well, that is all great, but I am not a pilot." I am with you. I am not a pilot either, but we can learn something from how these pilots checked their emotions. Negative people and circumstances come against any God-given dream. No matter how big or small our God-given dream, we *must* check our emotions before we can begin to GENERATE A PLAN. As the pilot of our God-given dream, doing an Emotional Check will take our dream to FLIGHT.

God's Plans

"For I know the plans I have for you," declares the Lord, "plans to prosper you and not to harm you, plans to give you hope and a future. Then you will call upon me and come and pray to me, and I will listen to you. You will seek me and find me when you seek me with all your heart. I will be found by you," declares the Lord. (Jer. 29:11-14a NIV)

How do we plan in the Lord? God has a plan for that too. I am no Biblical scholar. I am a person who endeavors to keep my Christian walk simple, yet productive. I am thankful that God's plan is as simple as following the instructions written in the above verses.

Calling on God, coming to Him, and praying while believing that He hears us, positions us to receive His plan. We will discover God's plan when we seek God. We seek God when we actively pursue Him by consistently reading His Word and spending time in prayer. Seeking God does not mean that we sit and do nothing but read our Bibles and pray. It does mean that we make a decision to spend time in fellowship with God daily. This discipline of fellowship with God will connect our heart to Him and position us to receive His plan. Then, when we need help planning, all we need to do is ask. God will not only listen to us, but He will help us to GENERATE A PLAN.

A plan not only keeps us on track day-to-day but helps stir up our hopes because, with a plan, we can see our God-given dream become a reality. This reality allows us to rest in peace, knowing that there is a completion. Choosing to bring into existence God's method to achieve our God-given dream helps us fulfill it.

CHART the Details

It is interesting what you learn along a journey. During that international flight to Cairo, a map of the world would periodically pop-up on the monitor in front of me. This interactive map displayed a little white airplane moving slowly to the east. The airplane seemed attached to a thread that connected dots that spanned across the Atlantic Ocean and several countries. As we moved through the air, this electronic icon moved along its charted course towards our final destination. Even if our airplane was to get a little off course, the course was there for us to go back to so that we could get to where we needed to be. For me, this visual captured what a plan is and how it works. We must GENERATE A PLAN in a similar way.

When planning, it is important to have a plan (as simple as that may sound). A vision is a dream picture of a destination, but a plan brings the details of how to get to the destination into focus. That electronic flight map detailed our course from beginning to end. When our pilot followed the details of the plan, we were able to stay on course.

A chart maps out a course. As we have been developing *Means* by connecting *Wings* to God-given dreams, God's plans for us have already begun to come into focus. We may not know all the details, but we must CHART the Details that we know.

CHART

Chronological tasks
Holding patterns
Agendas for meetings
Reachable milestones
Timeframes

Chronological tasks:

We now have the details - or *Dated Actions* - necessary to GENERATE A PLAN. All we need to do is put them in chronological order in our calendar (more on types of calendars in this chapter).

Holding patterns:

When an actual airplane comes in for its landing, it enters a holding pattern when it must wait for air traffic control to give it clearance to land or move forward. When we GENERATE A PLAN, we need to build in similar holding patterns so as not to stack tasks back-to-back but allow time for completion.

Agendas for meetings:

It is good to have an agenda, whether meeting with members of a team or simply by yourself (which, believe it or not, is a very productive thing to do if done right). In the next chapter, we will discuss how the acronym for FLIGHT also applies to meetings.

Reachable milestones:

We may not know all the dates and times of arrival at each stop along the way, but we must set the bigger stops in "stones." These milestones - written in our calendars - will help strengthen our resolve to move forward and help connect our tasks. If too far apart, these milestones can weaken rather than strengthen our resolve. Instead of encouraging us onward, the lack of viewable milestones can discourage us. When we place milestones evenly throughout our plan, however, we can not only see them, but we can reach them.

Timeframes:

A beginning and an end is what makes a plan a plan. We can say, "I plan on doing that," but, if there is not a beginning or end laid out, we do not have a plan - only an intention. Simply put, timeframes "frame" the timing of our work. Although the timing may change, when kept in a frame, our God-given dream will stay in focus.

Of course, it is important to CHART the Details, but we

also must connect those details to something that we can tangibly look at and manage. There are many tools available that can help us make this connection. Depending on the size of the plan, our tools could range from a 3 x 5 note card (which I use for weekly planning) to a multi-media management system. Below are three different tools that fit different plans and personalities.

1. Paper Plan

A pen-to-paper person may prefer using flip chart paper, legal pads, or 3 x 5 note cards to connect a plan to a calendar. Paper systems are good for people who are disciplined in keeping their papers organized. When using a paper planner, we must remember to keep track and view it as valuable. For the first-time planner, I recommend keeping the planner connected to an already valuable item, such as a purse or a set of keys. This connection will train one to protect their planner.

Although some people may consider a paper plan archaic, as long as there is paper around there will be people who choose this way of planning. It is always good to update and move forward; yet, if paper planning helps to "*Now finish the work!*" then stick with the plan that is working.

2. Typed Plan

Starting on paper and moving to a document can be useful to help a plan grow. When I began generating the plan for this book, I first started with a legal pad and then transcribed the plan into a spreadsheet that I could save for reference purposes. A typed plan may be better served when sharing with others. Just like any plan, a typed plan must be easily accessible, as well as simple. Too many graphics, pie charts, or words can limit the use of a plan. Typed plans lend themselves to be easily copied into an email or hand-held calendar. Of course, it is always important to "back up" anything valuable that is typed.

3. Cyber Plan

For those who like to share plans electronically, I recommend using project management software to aid in the generation of a plan. For longer and larger God-given dreams that have multiple people involved, these work great. When producing training videos for an international company, I found the cyber plan very useful. It gives people the option to print or electronically link individuals to the plan without them being able to adjust it. If this route is chosen, I highly recommend a program that links to calendar software. This way when *Dated Actions* are plugged in, they will directly merge into a personal calendar.

When we GENERATE A PLAN, it is so fun because we can mix it up, as long as we keep it connected. I work multiple plans at a time. Some of these originated on paper, some on a computer, and some online. The key is to connect plans to one chosen form. If a person works best with a paper calendar then, no matter how they CHART the Details, those details must make it into their personal paper calendar. Likewise, if a person uses online software to hold their calendar, it is imperative to sync up all plans generated in a notebook or another electronic device. In HAVE ACCOUNTABILITY, we will cover how to sync a plan so that our God-given dream can take to FLIGHT.

When we take our God-given dreams through the Pre-Check exercise, we will grow in the *Means* of GENERATE A PLAN. By conducting an Emotional Check, we safely secure our luggage; by committing to God's Plans, we secure our destination; and by applying CHART the Details, we secure and map our course.

While it is true that doing the Pre-Check brings security, there are times when turbulence tries to destroy God's plans. When outside pressure tries to break apart God's plans, what should we do?

Gate #8 - CONNECTOR QUESTION
"When do I just *Wing It*?"

Maneuver: The Power of Lift

God's Word is the *Wings* that give the lift to our FLIGHT, which means that the law of lift supersedes the laws of our plans. God is the Creator. He not only created us, but He created "The Way" in which we live on this planet. It is interesting to look at the parallel of the laws of the science of flying alongside the spiritual laws that help us take our God-given dreams to FLIGHT.

The lift of an airplane occurs most often because of a

turning of a flow of air mainly in relationship to wings. We can group this process into three parts: object, motion, and air. When we consider the "object," its shape and size are the primary factors. When we consider "motion," its velocity, or the measurement of the change, and degree of incline are key. When we consider "air," its amount and resistance, or strength, are principal. As an object moves, air resistance slows it down. The faster the object's motion, the greater the air resistance exerted against it. So, how does this translate into FLIGHT phraseology? Honestly I, myself, am on the edge of physics overload; but, when we apply these laws to the principles of FLIGHT, even I can see the connection.

Think about our God-given dream as the "object" - that dream can be big or small. As that dream takes to FLIGHT, "motion" or change occurs during takeoff, the flight itself, and the landing. During these ups and downs, our dream will encounter "air" resistance. All of these factors can most certainly affect our ability to get to our destination. However, there is no other factor that is more important to us when taking to FLIGHT than the connection we have to *Wings*.

Wings - the Word of God - bring the lift to our God-given dream, no matter its size. Whatever change occurs, *Wings* bring stability. However, *Wings* will not turn us in the right direction until we begin to move. Another way to look at this is that - we are the "object," our behavior is the "motion," and our speaking is the "air." These three components are important, but *Wings* give us the lifting power to soar towards our destination.

By our studying the Word of God and speaking the promises found in the Word of God, we will begin to know, hear, and act upon the plans that God has for us. Through this process, our faith is developed. The development of our faith is vital to our taking our God-given dreams to FLIGHT. When storms come, or when jetlag tries to set in, we will have the faith to *Wing It!*

Maintenance: Faith in *Wings*

***"So then faith comes by hearing,
and hearing by the word of God."
(Rom. 10:17 NKJV)***

The more we spend time with God - in Word and prayer, the more our faith in His *Wings* develops. I know this truth because I have experienced situations where - had I not developed faith to *Wing It!* my God-given dream would have crashed. This very book is a good example of a *Wing It!* scenario.

This book's rough draft was three-fourths complete when, after almost four years in the making, my FLIGHT hit a large storm. It is helpful to understand a little of the FLIGHT book background prior to the turbulence. A year after God called me to step away from my career, He began to give form to two writing projects that He wanted me to focus on - FLIGHT being one of them. For the first few years, we made some drastic lifestyle changes to help me fulfill this call, which included downsizing our house and selling many of our belongings to pay off debt. Also, my husband gave up his career as a freelancer for video production to take a corporate job with more stability in schedule and pay.

Over the next year, God gave us specific instructions in other areas of our lives. Already working on my life as a devoted wife and mother, God called me to home-school our children, as well as launch and lead a field trip organization. During this same time, God placed it in our hearts to take on the additional responsibility as co-leaders of a video ministry department, as well as to join the staff of our church. All the while and for the next three years, God helped me GENERATE A PLAN so that I was able to research, study, and begin FLIGHT, the book project.

Financially, our provision came through my husband's job, which allowed me to continue teaching, writing, and coordinating ministry and other activities - and then that plan seemingly began to fall apart. My husband, who had earned many promotions and accolades over the years, now faced a season of financial drought. During this time, we cinched up every area of our stewardship that we knew how to keep moving forward with the plans that God had given us. Then, one day, I got the call that my husband had been laid off and, more specifically, with no severance package. When he got home that day, we both looked at one another…and smiled! Just a few years prior to this, we had made a commitment to trust God at His Word - no matter what happened. This challenge was our time to *Wing It!* so that we could keep taking to FLIGHT.

For the next several months, I often entertained thoughts

of me returning to the corporate world. I knew, however, that God had called me to stay home, teach, and finish this book, along with other projects. Months went by and still no job. We pulled from savings and investments to keep bills paid, and our life moving forward, all the while continuing to put FLIGHT to paper.

With all our might, we still could not meet our needs; thank God, He never asks us to.

"And my God shall supply all your need according to His riches in glory by Christ Jesus." (Phil. 4:19 NKJV)

During this time, friends and family showered us with blessings. Very generous, anonymous donations that came to us as a direct answer to prayers paid most of our financial obligations. God met our needs and even our wants week in and week out. Week-by-week, day-by-day, we allowed His *Wings* to lift our FLIGHT to heights that we could not even imagine.

Stalling out is the easy thing to do when our God-given dream meets resistance, but moving forward is what will allow God to make up the distance. Keeping focused on writing this book did not make sense, because the book was not producing tangible fruit at the time. However, God's *Wings* and the plan that He helped me generate lifted and positioned me to stay the course. It was during those months that FLIGHT, the book, gained its widest momentum.

Faith is evident in the things we do not see.[7] When God calls, and we respond, our faith and God's *Wings* can lift and position us above any circumstance. It is in this position that we can soar (while making up for any loss) and reach our destination. As we keep pressing on with God, that tilt allows *Wings* to soar us out of the storm. Forward motion, whether on an airplane or as we work our FLIGHT plan, keeps us in the air so that we can use *Wings* to get beyond the dark clouds and turbulent times.

In both good and bad times, we have to be willing to *Wing It!* The bottom line is this: without the Word of God, we are people flapping our arms who will eventually grow tired and fall. So, how do we balance to GENERATE A PLAN with the decision to *Wing It!* so that we can keep taking to FLIGHT? It comes down to not trusting in the plan but trusting in "The One" who helped us bring it into existence. That is why it is so important to involve God.

You might be thinking, "Wow, I have messed up. I have been planning instead of involving God to help me GENERATE A PLAN." You might even be in a plan right now that you charted yourself in your strength and are flapping your arms to try and make it work. Well, let me encourage you that it is never too late to GENERATE A PLAN with God.

When I arrived in Cairo, Egypt, I began working my plan and flapping my arms. Once I let go of my plan and began to work the plan God already had for me - I experienced lift. You see, I thought that I was on that trip to do the work of my company, but I truly believe that God switched my plans from Canada to

Cairo for me to reconnect with Him. He took me to a place where, centuries before, His people had become slaves to work, plans were no longer being generated, and "the same old way of doing things" was tolerated. He showed me the riverbank where a little boy's mother - the mother of Moses - had faith in God's *Wings* to lift her family right out of the worst kind of turbulence. He took me to the largest tombs ever erected - the great pyramids - and showed me how the plans of men, however successful, are not fulfilling. That trip changed my life. It was during that trip that I began turning my life back to God and His Word. From that time on, with many mistakes along the way, I began pursuing God's plans instead of my own.

I am not perfect, but none of us are, which is why we should *Wing It!* when we GENERATE A PLAN. Have a plan, work that plan, and all the while allow God to work with and through that plan by trusting in His *Wings*. In doing so, our lives will become better as we develop the *Means* of FLIGHT.

We gain focus when we trust God and His Word to fulfill our plan. What comes next, however, will determine if we fulfill our God-given dream.

We have learned that we should never plan but instead GENERATE A PLAN. When we GENERATE A PLAN, we bring into existence a method to achieve an end. Once we have that plan, we can trust in God and receive the "lift" that He gives His *Wings*. Let us review the *Means* of:

<u>GENERATE A PLAN</u>

Gate #6 - CONNECTOR QUESTION
"Why *GENERATE A PLAN?*"

Maneuver: *Wings* to God-given dreams
Maintenance: Connect it, don't push it

Gate #7 - CONNECTOR QUESTION
"How do I *'Pre-Check'* the plan?"

Maneuver: The Pre-Check
Maintenance: Emotional Check, God's Plans, CHART the Details

Gate #8 - CONNECTOR QUESTION
"When do I just *Wing It*?"

Maneuver: The Power of Lift
Maintenance: Faith in *Wings*

We have begun to develop the *Means* of GENERATE A PLAN. It is time to "*Now finish the work!*" and complete this flight. This In-FLIGHT Check will help us get to where God knows that we can be. It is true that with the right **planning** we can…

Develop *Means* by Connecting *Wings* to God-Given Dreams

In-FLIGHT Check

Recording what we learn along the way will help us develop beyond today!

Develop *Means* of GENERATE A PLAN by answering this Connector Question: "Why GENERATE A PLAN?"

____

____

____

Develop *Means* of GENERATE A PLAN by answering this Connector Question: "How do I 'Pre-Check' the plan?"

Emotional Check:

____

____

____

God's Plans:

____

____

____

CHART the Details:

____

____

____

Develop *Means* of GENERATE A PLAN by asking this Connector Question, "When do I just *Wing It?*"

____

____

____

Connecting *Wings* of **planning**: Seek God and write out Scriptures that lift the answer to the above questions.

____

____

____

____

Now it is time for us to roll-up our sleeves and take action as the development of our FLIGHT climbs to an "*attitude*" where we must HAVE ACCOUNTABLITY.

For reapplication use printable versions of the In-FLIGHT Check pages, go to the link below to access these and other resources:

www.yourflightplans.com/tools

Chapter Five

HAVE ACCOUNTABILITY

Some things just do not fit - like a lady dressed in overalls in attendance at an executive meeting. I did not intend for my first impression to be so...comfortable. There I sat at a table surrounded by businessmen and women dressed like "Annie Get Your Gun" (minus the weapon) thinking, "This is not my fault."

Standing in my hotel room, while staring at my clothing options, I made a decision. I convinced myself that I deserved to let loose and wear something comfortable as I journeyed to my next new home away from home. I had traveled for several weeks to multiple cities with no downtime. I persuaded myself that I needed to get comfortable so that I could enjoy the next few flights. My assistant had made arrangements for me to fly separately from my colleagues. The plan was for me to leave earlier, so that I had longer layovers, ensuring peaceful connectors along the way. I snubbed my nose at my business attire and neatly placed it in my suitcase. I then pulled out my victory flight suit, aka an old pair of blue jean overalls that I had recently purchased for a team-building outing.

I laughed at my attempt at being casual as I caught a glimpse of myself in a mirror walking out of the hotel towards my company rental car. A little voice on the inside of me said that I had gone too far. I shook my head at that little voice saying, "I am one of the most 'creased' employees at my company. I always represent the company well. I have seen people dress more casual than this as they travel straight to their job sites. I am traveling alone. I cannot remember the last time that I was home. I do not even know what city I am leaving because I have been in so many lately that they are running together. I deserve this! I am wearing my overalls and my tennis shoes, and that's it." Then, I threw my suitcase in the trunk and my briefcase onto the passenger seat, buckled up, and headed to the airport.

Proud that I had a perfect record for my luggage arriving on time, I smugly checked my suitcase and proceeded to my plane. Accompanied by a small purse and briefcase, my attire (although foreign to me) seemed to set me free. After boarding, I even reclined my seat a little before the flight attendant gave us clearance. I felt like a new woman.

While asleep in flight, I was awakened by turbulence. Soon following was the announcement I did *not* want to hear. Our flight was being diverted to another city (not just any city but Houston, Texas, one of the largest cities in America). Once we landed, we were informed that we had to change planes. They assured us our luggage would make that change as well.

For the next few hours, I waited with dozens of strangers for the storm to pass so that our flight could takeoff. Very late in the evening, our plane received clearance, and we headed to the location printed on our tickets. For me, that was merely another connector to my final destination.

We were the last plane landing that night at the Dallas-Ft. Worth Airport (which is saying a lot considering that based on square miles, it is the size of a small city). As we made our way to the terminal area, we were greeted by an attendant who shared with us that there were no more flights leaving the airport. She encouraged us that we could choose to stay in the safety of the airport facilities, or they would provide us with a room nearby. Even in overalls, I preferred a bed as opposed to sharing a row of plastic chairs with my new friends; so, I followed the attendant to the desk. While standing in line, a voice over the intercom system shared with us that our luggage had not yet arrived. Apparently this small city had one less airplane than anticipated, which happened to be the one carrying my suitcase.

I spent the next hour in line filling out my claim's paperwork. I then grabbed my complimentary bag of miniature toothpaste and other tiny-sized toiletries and caught the shuttle to my hotel. Soon after I crawled into bed, my wake-up call sounded. My three-hour nap had come to an end, and I was headed out to greet the shuttle for my return trip to the airport.

My "two-day-old overalls" and I caught a red-eye flight bound for the East Coast of America, hopeful for a strong tailwind and an early arrival time. As my plane slowed down in mid-flight due to a storm, I was yet again delayed from arriving on schedule.

By the time I landed, my team had sent someone to pick me up and take me directly to the business meeting. No amount of caffeine or deodorant could change what I had chosen to wear the day before. As I walked in, I greeted a group of clients that, for the next few weeks, I was charged with the job of supporting, training, mentoring, and inspiring. All I could do was smile and make a joke about how I had just come from a rural town in the Midwestern United States.

I had good intentions, but I was still late and underdressed. Even though I did not make excuses outwardly, inside I refused to own up (in my view, I had done nothing wrong).

Being accountable is the willingness to accept responsibility for one's actions;[1] that then positions us to take ownership of those very actions. For this reason, taking to FLIGHT requires more than our intention to show up but also to "own up." Our ownership of our God-given dream will determine whether we just "have" a dream or whether we "fulfill" a dream. Once we take responsibility for our actions, we can produce the results needed to take our God-given dream to FLIGHT.

Productivity is generated through accountability.

Taking to FLIGHT is fun, exciting, and full of passion and accomplishments, but it is nothing if we do not generate

productivity.

To HAVE ACCOUNTABILITY, we must remind ourselves, as many times as needed, to "whom" we are to be accountable. When God gives us a dream, He needs us to fulfill it - He needs us to produce - He needs us to HAVE ACCOUNTABILITY.

Thank God that because we are willing to fly on *Wings* of **productivity**, He is now able to help us HAVE ACCOUNTABILITY. Let's put on our FLIGHT goggles because we are going where few have gone before: not into the wild blue yonder but higher than most are willing to travel. We are going to an *attitude* where we can develop the *Means* of HAVE ACCOUNTABILITY.

Gate #9 - CONNECTOR QUESTION
"What is my approach?"

Maneuver: The "UP" Factor

Our approach will set the pace of our relationship. Our approach to HAVE ACCOUNTABILITY does not have to be perfect, but it must be consistently productive. I believe it is the "UP" factor that makes a huge difference whether we live a fulfilling life or not. We can own, know, and grow in our personal development, but without the "UP" factor, we simply have no lift. So, what does it mean to own, know, and grow-UP to HAVE ACCOUNTABILITY? This factor is where our approach begins.

Maintenance: Own-UP, Know-UP, Grow-UP

Own-UP

Own-UP, Know-UP, and Grow-UP are always two-fold operations. For example, when we Own-UP, we admit to God, ourselves, our teams, and possibly others that this dream is not just ours but one that was God-given. It is not prideful to Own-UP but rather respectful. Pride would be taking credit for a dream that we did not create, but respect is giving God credit and honor for the dream that He gave to us. For this reason, "Own" is taking responsibility according to our *Means*, while "UP" is giving God the glory as He gives us the *Wings* to reach our destination.

There have been many times in my life that I have owned something but did not Own-UP. This perspective came to me during one of my personal moments of developing the *Means* of FLIGHT. I went through a challenge as I embarked on the HAVE ACCOUNTABILITY section of a personal, God-given dream. As I share my struggles and victories, hopefully, we will all find encouragement.

Years ago, while flying between cities on a business trip, God placed a dream inside my heart - a dream to write a book. At the time, I was young(er), and I allowed my ego to have a voice regarding how to go about making this dream come true. I have always been a hard worker, so this idea of mine (which was my first mistake) began to consume me. At the time, I was traveling from city to city working with elite businessmen and women who were constantly seeking my advice. For a young, driven, career-minded person, I was living the high life. Writing a book seemed like the right thing to do, considering "I" had all this knowledge to help people.

Naturally (not spiritually), I began formulating my notes and planning my strategy for this great book I was to produce. Time and time again, I came up with good, short bursts of composition, but I had no glue to bind them together. Over a period of years, I gained pockets of ideas that I knew would collectively make a great book, but I still kept coming up short in the area of production. I even took one of those ideas and created a successful management class around it, but I still kept hitting a wall as to how to pull those ideas together into a book.

There were many times that I beat myself up because I had failed to produce a book. The real truth is that the reason I kept failing was because I did not Own-UP this God-given dream.

We fail to Own-UP when we do and plan a dream instead of discovering and generating it. I had decided to write a book; in doing so, I sidestepped the important developments of the *Means* of FORWARD THINKING and GENERATE A PLAN. While it was and is true that God placed a desire to write on my heart, it was not my place to take that desire and force it into my plan.

Once I humbled myself, I began to recognize, through much time in His Word and prayer, God gave me this dream to write a book. For this reason, I needed to give Him the credit and to seek His counsel actively in every area of this dream. I found direction and encouragement in God's Word to Jeremiah:

> ***"For I know the plans I have for you," declares the Lord, "plans to prosper you and not to harm you, plans to give you hope and a future. Then you will call upon me and come and pray to me, and I will listen to you. You will seek me and find me when you seek me with all your heart. I will be found by you," declares the Lord.***
> ***(Jer. 29:11-14a NIV)***

When we try to own something that is not ours, it can cause undue stress in our lives and added pressure to complete or finish what we have begun. I believe that much of the stress in multiple areas of our lives comes from trying to own dreams, concepts, ideas, and plans that were truly never ours.

Our ownership sounds so familiar since we have already flown through FORWARD THINKING. Own-UP, however, must not simply be a beginning approach but rather one that carries on through the fulfillment of a God-given dream. Seeking God in the area of our dreams must be an ongoing approach as we learn to "let go" of that part of us that wants the credit for the success that we so yearn to accomplish. The good news is that if we fail in our approach and come to God with a pure heart, His *Wings* will lift us back on course.

God promises to lead us out of the captivity of our mistakes when we Own-UP. Once I was able to get myself out of the ownership mentality, I was able to Own-UP, which allowed me to go to the next level of HAVE ACCOUNTABILITY.

Know-UP

Having developed an Own-UP mindset, I then recognized that my knowledge alone would not take my God-given dream the distance. Gaining knowledge from God about how to actively pursue the dream had a lot to do with getting myself out of the way. You see, for years I had relied on what I knew; this self-reliance is quite the opposite of the Know-UP approach. When we rely on what we know, we limit God from taking us *beyond* our abilities.

"For I bear witness that according to their ability, yes, and beyond their ability, they were freely willing."
(2 Cor. 8:3 NKJV)

For us to be accountable, we must first know that HAVE ACCOUNTABILITY comes from knowledge of the account we have been made able in. When we put our knowledge above God's knowledge, we set ourselves up to be the one who must account for all that we can know. God wants us to reach our destination, and so He urges us to chart our course in His direction so that He can fill us with the ability to know where to go. When we Know-UP, we obtain the ability to God's account.

Account: Debits and credits to cover transactions;
reason for action -statement of conduct, value,
importance, advantage[2]

Ability: Power to perform, competence in doing, skill[3]

When we know that we have God's account and the ability to perform, there is no outward storm or internal challenge that can get us off of our FLIGHT plan. When we consider God first, His consideration is our advantage.

God covers our transactions when we transact. I love the word "transaction." A transaction is an exchange or transfer of services between two parties.[4] If we are willing, the gifts inside of us are acceptable. Transactions with God include withdrawing knowledge from His Word. God expects and wants us to make withdrawals. When we actively seek God's knowledge, He can deposit it into our hearts so that it can then be relayed to our head - not the other way around.

For years, I tried to understand how to use my gifts, but it was not until I pursued God's Word and sought Him with all my heart that I learned what my next steps were. The heart houses our motives. Knowledge of what to do or where to go or who to involve must start from a God-motive if we want to live a life fulfilled and not just one of success.

Knowledge helps to ignite us so that we can take to FLIGHT. When we Know-UP, the flame inside of us (our God-given dream) will spark. Our excitement will match the completion of the arrival to our destination. HAVE ACCOUNTABILITY is not just about taking to FLIGHT, but it is about getting to where God knows that we can be.

So, once we begin with God, we must be willing to finish with God. What we know can consume us, but our relying on what God knows allows the fire inside of our God-given dream to go "up" instead of "out."

Grow-UP

We can Own-UP and Know-UP, but if we do not Grow-UP, we will never go "up." Just like an aircraft must have an order to its flight, our approach must also have order. We cannot Grow-UP until we Own-UP and Know-UP. If you are alive you grow, that is a fact. But not everything that is alive will grow up. Many plants grow out, and some even grow down, but until they grow up, there can be no real produce. Potatoes are just a root until they sprout and produce other potatoes. I am no potato, and hopefully neither are you, so how about we Grow-UP so we can produce something that will take to FLIGHT instead of continually be grounded.

Grow-UP is the one term out of the three that may lead to stepping on toes…not just potatoes. This risk of offense is because it requires us to get real about where we are in our development. To Own-UP and Know-UP puts the pressure on God simply by acknowledging Him as "The Source" to all we have and do. However, to Grow-UP puts the pressure on us to receive and do all that He has given us through His account - or does it?

When we Grow-UP we must do it in a way that keeps us moving forward and enjoying the trip while reaching our destination. How do we Grow-UP through HAVE ACCOUNTABILITY without crashing under the pressure? I don't have all of the answers, but hopefully my sharing some of the self-induced turbulence I have experienced will encourage you to embrace the Grow-UP approach.

The term Grow-UP can spark different topics, but to keep it simple and in the realm of FLIGHT, it comes down to one word: discipline. To Grow-UP, we all must apply discipline in FLIGHT. God gave us our dreams; for this reason, He will also give us the discipline required for us to Grow-UP to fulfill them.

The topic of discipline reminds me of the first year I began putting this book FLIGHT to paper (or rather computer screen). I was so excited to get started on this book, but then God assigned me another writing project. God called me to create a website and to begin posting articles twice a week in areas that I was developing in through His Word.

I did not like this approach. This approach was not part of my plan. I did not want to share my day-to-day personal growing-up in the things of the Lord for all to read and ponder on. I did not want to take time away from my long awaited dream of writing

this book. Two words: Grow-UP. I began to remember how my approach, years before regarding producing a book, did not yield any fruit. So I quickly agreed to God's plan and asked Him how to go about developing the discipline to fulfill it. God showed and taught me, as I humbled myself to His approach, what to do daily and weekly that would allow me to "*Now finish the work!*"

Just like each FLIGHT plan is different, the discipline required to fulfill the plan will be different for each one of us. How God calls us to do something is as unique as what He calls each one of us to do. Our ability to discern these differences is one of the reasons why our relationship with the Lord is so important. I could share with you the discipline it took to write this book, but the discipline that you need to fulfill your God-given dream will not look the same. I can tell you this: when we Own-UP, Know-UP, and Grow-UP, God will reveal to each of us individually exactly what we need to do to fulfill our FLIGHT plan.

Beyond specific disciplines that He will teach, guide, or lead us to, there are some basic maneuvers that can help steer our FLIGHT plans along the way. These basic Maneuvers and Maintenance can be applied to all God-given dreams because they are fundamental to HAVE ACCOUNTABILITY. So, I humbly share these disciplines from my tool box that I have learned along the way from my Heavenly Father, the Master

Mechanic.

Maneuver: Monday Mornings and Beyond

Often, Monday mornings are a jumping off point for our work week; for this reason, maintaining the development of the *Means* of FLIGHT goes beyond day one. Remember: "Productivity is generated through accountability." Here are some practical approaches that produce no matter what day of the week it may be.

Maintenance: Meetings and Mechanics

Meetings

Throughout my career in training and development, I implemented, executed, and led many meetings - from conference calls to webinars to meetings with employees or leadership. Some of my most productive meetings were during the years that I supervised the opening of restaurants. When you have approximately ninety days to open a multi-million dollar investment, it is important to maximize your time. During that short timeframe, multiple meetings would take place between heads of departments including construction, operations, training, and even local city officials. These meetings were critical in the communication of the project. That experience has been such a blessing to me, because I learned practices that worked and those that did not. I gleaned the principles I learned in that position and brought them forward into my role as a consultant, as well as other leadership roles.

Along the way, I was reminded of the most important things to remember when it comes to meetings. Meetings are important, but if unbalanced, meetings can choke a vision.

It is essential to balance the fuel on an airplane. Too much fuel and the weight will not be distributed which can cause challenges. Too little fuel and the airplane will not be able to reach its destination safely. Meetings are the fuel between each stop. When meetings are timely and productive, the stops along the way to our destination will be less stressful. Successful meetings are those that follow:

FLIGHT

- **FORWARD THINKING** - Does the meeting have a vision? What is the purpose of the meeting and has it been communicated to those attending?

- **LINK ACTIONS TO IDEAS** - The purpose behind the meeting should be driven by three-to-five specific goals that will move that meeting to action. Discuss those topics and link actionable steps that will follow the meeting.

- **INVOLVE THOSE NEEDED** - Ask yourself:
  1. CALL - Who needs to attend this meeting? The purpose of the meeting will determine its attendance.
  2. CONSIDER - What should the meeting accomplish? Communicate expectations in advance to those

attending so they know what to bring and what their role is during the meeting.

3. CARRY - How much time should I allow for each topic? Allocate time to discuss each goal topic and stay within the timeframe. It is helpful to have someone other than the meeting facilitator take notes during the meeting to have a consistent record of what was discussed.

- **GENERATE A PLAN** - Set milestones and specific next steps, with dates attached. Avoid the details and focus on a 20,000-foot level approach. Imagine the view from an airplane's window while at 20,000 feet: you will only be able to see the large geographical spots on the land, as well as what is ahead and behind the plane. We should apply this "big picture" approach to each of our meetings.

- **HAVE ACCOUNTABILITY** - Everyone should be accountable to someone for individual accomplishments. "Productivity is generated through accountability."

- **THANKSGIVING** - Make time for praise reports. Meetings are a unique time when productive people come together under a plan bigger than themselves. It is important to not miss an opportunity to encourage one another.

To keep meetings productive:

- **Have regular meetings about regular topics**
  If the plan being worked is driven by four or five agenda items,

then the team should regularly meet to discuss those specific areas. Once this pattern is established, over time, everyone will become used to the meeting dates, times, and agendas and will develop the team to honor the meetings.

- **Ask ourselves if these regular topics still apply**

For big projects like starting a business or producing a television series, there should be recurring meetings that continue for years. While it is true that some things vital to the vision never change, it is important to keep the meetings relevant and current. Change may need to happen, but before it does, it is important first to pray about it because God sees the end and the beginning.[5]

Mechanics

Practically, we need the nuts and bolts to keep things working; taking our God-given dream to FLIGHT is no different. While meetings involve others, here are three Mechanics that we can personally tighten up to HAVE ACCOUNTABILITY.

- **Write it down**

When we write something down it gets done, right? Well... sort of. I used to know someone that called herself the "Post-it Note Queen" and she fit that description. Her desk was covered with waves of pastel and fluorescent squares. Although she had disciplined herself to write everything down, she had not disciplined herself to look, do, or even remember half the time where she put a note. Can writing on little sticky papers and putting them all over be productive? Yes. All kinds of note taking can be productive if we apply HAVE ACCOUNTABILITY to it. Here are some questions to ask when developing a system for writing things down.

Will I discipline myself to revisit the place where I wrote and posted the note to myself?

If we do not ask this question, we may create unique wallpaper for our walls, mirrors, desks, or planners instead of a productive system. The method by which our records of *Dated Actions*, notes, important phone numbers, reoccurring important celebration days, and other information that helps to move a God-given dream forward depends a lot on personality.

There are many choices in planners (from handheld electronic devices to planners with calendars and to-do lists, to binders or legal pads) any of which can help in the area of HAVE ACCOUNTABILITY. The most important thing is not the "thing" used but how effective our system of using it is. I have witnessed the alarms for computer software calendars turn into just another background sound and planners collecting dust on a nightstand. I have heard the phrase, "The best planner is the one that you will use," but I see it differently.

The best planner is the one that will help you be the most productive.

In high school and college, I used a big planner and wrote everything down. While this did help me get a lot of things completed, I also wasted a lot of time. My personality lends itself to being very detailed; I would practically write short stories in my planner regarding dates, projects, and assignments. It would take so much time to sort through my planner at the beginning of each day that I would spend hours planning - leaving little time to work the plan.

Finally, I searched out planners and ended up designing my own to complement my personality. Since that time, I have found a balance in writing things down and have increased in productivity.

Are my notes geographically close enough to help me to fulfill them while also complementing other notes that I have written?

For years, I have kept a note card in my planner of a list of acknowledgments that need written by one of the departments I helped lead at my church. I would write down names of businesses or individuals that we would like to thank that month. I then would put down a *Dated Action* in my planner for a day to complete those thank you cards. Once I had written the note, I would tear up that note card and replace it with a new one for the next month or extended period. This system for collecting valuable information helped to move our department towards its destination. Of course, this system works just as well using a phone or electronic device (without tearing it up, of course).

- **Review and Preview**

Pick a day (that should be the last day of the week) to review the previous week and generate a plan for the week ahead. I learned this discipline from a corporate vice president I supported, who later became a chief learning officer for a Fortune 500 company. He taught me - "*An hour of reflection could change one's direction.*"

There are lessons to be learned from our review whether our week was productive or just busy. When we take that hour (or even thirty minutes) to review and apply what we have learned, we catch a preview of what we can accomplish in the week ahead.

As I sought God regarding this discipline, I learned that by applying some *Creatively Specific* additions I was able to HAVE ACCOUNTABILITY even more in this area. Here are some questions or statements that I began considering as I did review and preview.

What did I accomplish with God last week?

This is a great question to ask each week when we review the previous week in our planners. Remember, there is no condemnation for what we did not accomplish with God.[5] The bolt to tighten up is what we learned from our time management. When we get a better understanding of our priorities, then we can keep the next week focused on the right things instead of the urgent things that steal our time. Once I began to ask this question, I learned that I had not been accomplishing what I had initially intended on fulfilling. By asking this question, we move from a place of good intention to a place of productivity.

I will pray and thank God that I hear His voice, increase in learning, and that I am a person of understanding.[6]

This declaration puts us in a position to review from God's point of view instead of our own. We must remember that God has good plans for us, and He, more than anyone, wants us to fulfill those plans. This declaration helps to remind us that we do hear our Father, we are teachable, and as we write down a plan, we do so with wisdom.

Follow through on *Dated Actions* and commitments.

HAVE ACCOUNTABILITY means we as leaders are responsible for asking questions and requesting production. For this reason, we should plan to call those who are helping us. We should not simply look at what we need to do, but we should also GENERATE A PLAN to lead, guide, and encourage as the Lord has guided us through INVOLVE THOSE NEEDED. Then, in those areas that we are helping others fulfill their God-given dreams, we should be responsible for keeping our word to attend meetings, finish projects, and fulfill responsibilities that lend themselves to HAVE ACCOUNTABILITY.

- **Outbox My Inbox** *(empty our boxes so that we can fulfill our day)*
  "Where do I begin?" If this question comes to mind every

time we look at our emails or physical inboxes, we should not log off. When we look at all that is in our inboxes, we can become overwhelmed. Those little boxes do not have to rule us if we put some "rulers" in place to help keep us in line.

Ruler #1 - Two-Minute Touch

If we can touch it or click it and take care of it in two minutes or less, do it. Most of the time that we spend going through our inboxes is spent retouching the same papers or emails over and over.

Ruler #2 - Two Choices

Should I keep it or delete it? When we look at our inboxes, we simply need to ask this question and make a decision. We do not need to be bogged down by decisions that are over-complicated.

Ruler #3 - Action or Information

If we decide to keep it, then we should leave it or put it where we can retrieve it. It should stay in our inboxes if we need to take action within twenty-four hours. If it is going to take more time than that, then it is information that we should create a folder for and file it so as to reference it later.

Ruler #4 - Folders and Files Buy Back the Miles

Most people keep everything in their inbox convincing themselves that they have to do so to find it later. If these same people would simply take the time to put things in order, then they could replace repetitive keystrokes with less than a one-minute exploration of information that helps them get to their destination.

If we take the time to create a folder and a file within that folder to house the paperwork, then we can buy back time. This time can be used later when we need to retrieve that information.

We reap what we sow. If we do not take the time to establish an easy system to retrieve information, then we will harvest stress and frustration when we go to try to find it later.

Ruler #5 - A Good System of Order Keeps Us from Being Hoarders

It is easier to trash a whole file or folder than to have to look through mounds of information. Either every four, six, or twelve months, we should go through our folders and purge what we do not need. It helps if we put this action into our planner, so we do not forget to purge our folders. If we do not plan to purge, there will come a day that we will become overwhelmed by how many folders there are to sift through. When questioned, people throw out the whole system because they think it is too complicated. The real truth is that it simply was not managed properly.

Ruler #6 - Revisit #1-5 to Keep the System Alive

We are all a "work in progress" so we should not get discouraged when we notice that our inboxes are piling up. We should simply refresh our steps and remind ourselves of why we are applying these rulers.

We do not want to have our inboxes rule us; for this reason, we must apply rulers to keep us in line. Keeping this system alive by revisiting these rulers helps us HAVE ACCOUNTABILITY.

The practicalities of developing the *Means* of HAVE ACCOUNTABILITY are found in the every day approaches that we take to keep us moving toward our destinations. We can only move beyond Mondays when we apply practical approaches to Meetings and Mechanics. When we do this, we generate productivity through accountability.

No matter what God-given dream we are working on taking responsibility for, our actions lead us to a place of productivity. When we are willing to Own-UP, Know-UP, and Grow-UP, we can tighten up our Monday Mornings and Beyond. Let us review the FLIGHT approach of HAVE ACCOUNTABILITY.

HAVE ACCOUNTABILITY

Gate #9 - CONNECTOR QUESTION
"What is my approach?"

Maneuver: The "UP" Factor

Maintenance: Own-UP, Know-UP, Grow-UP

Maneuver: Monday Mornings and Beyond
Maintenance: Meetings and Mechanics

HAVE ACCOUNTABILITY helps us to "*Now finish the work!*" This In-FLIGHT Check will help us get to where God knows that we can be. It is true that our approach to **productivity** can help us…

Develop *Means* by Connecting *Wings* to God-Given Dreams

<u>In-FLIGHT Check</u>

Recording what we learn along the way will help us develop beyond today!

Develop *Means* of HAVE ACCOUNTABILITY by answering this Connector Question: "What is my approach?" Remember:

Productivity is generated through accountability.

Own-UP, Know-UP, Grow-UP:

____

____

____

____

____

____

Meetings:

F ____

L ____

I ____

G ____

H ____

T ____

Mechanics:

- Write it Down

____

____

____

- Review and Preview

____

____

____

____

- Outbox My Inbox (Rulers)

____

____

____

____

____

____

Connecting *Wings* of **productivity**: Seek God and write out Scriptures that lift the answer to the above questions.

____

____

____

____

____

We have traveled through ***A Time to Create*** and
A Time to Generate, and now we are ready to explore
A Time to Celebrate. Let us gain refreshment
as we develop the *Means* of THANKSGIVING.

For reapplication use printable versions
of the In-FLIGHT Check pages,
go to the link below to access these and other resources:

www.yourflightplans.com/tools

A Time to Celebrate

Celebrate: to honor[1]

A Time to Celebrate takes us from our in FLIGHT celebration to the gateway of our destination. Developing the *Means* of THANKSGIVING will give us ideas on how to honor or refresh the God-given dream inside of us while encouraging our travel companions along the way.

When we look back, we will not reflect on all of the work that it took to develop the *Means* of FLIGHT, but we will remember the **pleasure** that helped us to fulfill our God-given dream.

Chapter Six

THANKSGIVING

I did not second guess my decision to fly with two young children to visit my mom until about the second hour of being stuck on the ground in a plane during a lightning storm. We were coming off of a relaxing trip to Florida when, on the first leg of our return flight home, we realized why the Sunshine State is known as the Lightning Capital of America. During a severe electrical storm, a commercial airplane must land and, once on the ground, remain immobile until given clearance for departure. While this was good information to know, it was not so enjoyable to experience first-hand.

Our flight was directed to land at a nearby airport to wait out the storm. Our aircraft was not cleared to deplane; for this reason, the favor we received from the flight crew was a breath of fresh air. One of the crew members kneeled down next to me and shared that although we would not be able to enter the terminal, no one said we could not play on the jet bridge. My little passengers were ready to run, and so was I! For the next fifteen minutes or so, my two very energetic children and I played tag in what, as far as we knew, was an authorized area. The crew smiled as they waved us back into the airplane to prepare for departure. Our appreciation was mutual. We all knew that little recess was simply a decision made for the greater good.

Catching my breath as the plane ascended towards the sky, all anticipation of a restful ride shattered when the little man seated on my lap started to cry. Of course, this was not one of those sweet, soft cries you hear from the likes of a whimpering puppy having a little dream. No! My son's cry was a full blown, "I am exhausted, and everyone is going to know it!" type of cry. Everyone did know it, and we did not enjoy it, especially his sister who kept telling me so. At that moment, I wished I was in a rainforest on a mission field with my husband instead of this air-conditioned, metal echo chamber flying at 20,000 feet above the earth.

Praying, bouncing, cuddling, correcting, and shushing - nothing seemed to work - until the nice man came by with that heavenly cart containing a bucketful of frozen miracles. "Two orange juices," I spoke loudly over my screaming child. As I passed one to my daughter, out of the corner of my eye, I caught a glimpse of my son's little hand reaching to pull a chip of ice from my cup. You could almost hear the sighs of relief from the passengers and the angels in heaven weeping as his little fingers put that clear, dripping, ice crystal in between his red lips. A few moments later that same crew member came back with another cup - filled just with ice chips. He, too, had heard the same sighs of relief and heavenly voices rejoicing.

"Keep them coming," was all I could say. For the rest of that flight, I fed multiple cups of chipped ice to my crying eighteen-month-old son as I cradled him in my lap. Unlike the other passengers on the plane, my six-year-old daughter had decided to tune out the cries by looking out her window. As for me, I was just giving thanks that ice had finally been the pacifier needed to calm my son.

Our flight was a little easier because the environment had been refreshed. I wondered how many other situations the crew provided such pleasure towards on that very same flight.

It is so true that, from relay races to cups of icy goodness, the **pleasure** experienced on that flight was the direct result of the purposeful services others were willing to give. THANKSGIVING is the *Means* to give thanks to those specific people who help us fulfill our God-given dream. We must be purposeful when developing the *Means* of THANKSGIVING. Answering this question will help us bring **pleasure** on purpose.

Gate #10 - CONNECTOR QUESTION
"Who, how, and when do we give thanks?"

Maneuver: Giving Thanks to Dream Teams

No matter how big or small our God-given dream, there is always a team pursuing that dream. Depending on the God-given dream, one could have lists of people on that Dream Team. But, whether that team is just you and God or multiple people, giving thanks refreshes everyone.

It is critical to prioritize THANKSGIVING within the plans of God. That being said, God should always be the number one member of our Dream Team. Once we have prioritized God, we are then able to give thanks to the team of people God aligns us with to help fulfill our God-given dream. These people are truly valuable members of our Dream Team! The members of our Dream Team should include:

Co-Pilots

Next to God, our immediate family should be our THANKSGIVING priority. I know that I could not have written this book or fulfilled any of the other FLIGHT plans that I have embarked on if it had not have been for my husband. When we take our God-given dream to FLIGHT, our spouses and children do not just go along for the ride. A key to having a fulfilling life is to realize and recognize the active involvement those closest to us have in our journey. My husband and children have sacrificed alongside me. Giving thanks to our Co-Pilots is a must.

Crew

INVOLVE THOSE NEEDED is not just a chapter in a book but a Crew of individuals who deserve our ongoing thanks. From partners to assistants, to employees, to volunteers, these people make taking God-given dreams to FLIGHT possible no matter what role they fulfill.

Passengers

Of course without these people, what is the point of taking a dream to FLIGHT? Passengers are the recipients of the service or gift that we provide for the purpose of our God-given dream. No matter what our dream is, there is someone, besides ourselves, who benefits from it. Crew and Passengers could share the same nametag, but, either way, they fulfill two very different roles and can be given thanks separately.

Ground Support

And then there are those folks - the financial, spiritual, and emotional encouragers - that help give stability from the ground-level for our dream to take to FLIGHT. Most of the time their roles are not active in or even onboard our trip; but, in many ways, they keep the God-given dreams of all of us moving forward. They deserve our thanks, many times over.

Once we have determined who we should be sending our thanks towards, we then need to see that they receive it. So, how and when do we give thanks? I am sure that there are books written on this topic alone. For this reason, I do not even pretend to try and cover, nor do I know, all the ins and outs of giving thanks. However, I would like to share with you what I have found to be very successful and fulfilling ways to give thanks bringing refreshment as we develop *Means* by connecting *Wings* to God-given dreams.

Maintenance: Six Thank-Full Refreshments, Blessings FLIGHT Log, Encourage Yourself

"Now thanks be to God who always leads us in triumph in Christ, and through us diffuses the fragrance of His knowledge in every place." (2 Cor. 2:14 NKJV)

Everyone needs refreshment. The more we receive it from God, the more we can give it away. Either given or received, here are Six Thank-Full Refreshments that bring **pleasure** to any God-given Dream Team.

Six Thank-Full Refreshments

1. Represent

We are the number one representative of our God-given dream. For this reason, we must set the standard for the air quality in our environment. Publically praising God actively shows others our priorities and encourages others to do the same. Such praise encourages an air space of humility and unity because it helps to disinfect any pressure of pride or disloyalty by keeping everyone breathing in the awesome goodness of God.

As an example, when I first joined the staff of our church I immediately noticed the refreshing air quality of our meetings and group activities. Our pastor diffuses a fragrance of encouragement, primarily because his allegiance is first to his relationship with the Lord. His thank-full attitude towards the Lord creates a place for all of us to see our journey through thank-filled eyes.

One of the first things we can sense is the air quality around us. This attitude is not limited to ministries. I have known several exceptional business owners and executives who, when entering a room, changed the air quality simply by permeating a Godly thank-fullness with every word that he/she spoke. We have all experienced the difference one leader can make. We know what it is like to join a team in which the air feels restrictive and so thick you could cut it with a knife. Such an atmosphere stifles the development of the *Means* of FORWARD THINKING, LINK ACTIONS TO IDEAS, INVOLVE THOSE NEEDED, HAVE ACCOUNTABILITY, as well as THANKSGIVING. The opposite is true when leaders give thanks to God so that they can refresh those around them and help a God-given dream arrive at its intended destination.

2. Prayer

"I thank my God upon every membrance of you."
(Phil. 1:3 NKJV)

Prayer is a power-packed way to refresh a Dream Team. When we pray over our God-given dream and its Dream Team, everyone can breathe easier.

I make it a commitment to not get involved or lead a team that I do not have the time to pray over. In the past, when I did not make prayer a priority, I noticed significant changes occur - the most of which was my devotion towards the particular dream or team. Prayer helps us stay focused. I have learned to start my day praying over God-given dreams and teams that I lead. Prayer helps me to remember the commitment that I have made to God and the people I serve.

3. Special Gifts

Over the years, I have received many gifts in association with the travels, companies, and organizations that I served. Those that I am most grateful for are the gifts that took extra thought or effort, not necessarily money, to put together.

I recall a time when I was leading a team during one Thanksgiving holiday. Knowing that we were all far away from our loved ones, the head of management for the company we were supporting invited us to spend the day with his family. The family welcomed us with open arms of love and food.

Another time, one of the employees at a restaurant I supported brought me a container filled with her family's crop of crushed leaves used as a dye for both hair and fine linens. Later,

I found out that the amount she gifted me took hours to prepare, and the leaves were hand-picked from the highest branches of the trees in her orchard.

Then there was the time that a team of managers that I trained found out that my husband had asked me to marry him. On the last day of their training seminar, they presented me with a little ornament of a boy kneeling while giving a ring to a young girl. That afternoon they smothered me with hugs, cards, and encouragement for all that they had learned throughout their time with me. That little ornament sat on my desk for years as a reminder of that team and those sweet memories.

Some of my most coveted gifts have come from my husband and children. They are three of the most generous people I know. While writing this book, my computer stopped working. I had backed up my work on a hard drive but was faced with the challenge of not having a computer to use for my writing, as well as no budget for replacing it. One day I went out to run errands and came home to find that my husband had bought me a computer with money we had set aside for sowing seeds. He had set it up and had it waiting for me - ready to use - on my desk. Words cannot express how this act of his investing in my God-given dream refreshed me. I remember also when my daughter had a desire to visit the Biltmore House in North Carolina. After years of reading about and looking at pictures of the famous Estate, we were able to add it to a family vacation agenda. As we were leaving the Biltmore Estate, my daughter gave me a little gift bag. Inside was a mug she had bought with her money as her way of saying, "Thank you." Many times as I write, I sip tea from that mug.

My son also has the sweetest ways of saying, "Thank you." Over the years, he has drawn me pictures and written me notes. One such note was a sweet card he wrote with the assistance of his sister when he was just four years old. I intend to hold on to this card for the rest of my life! These special gifts from my family bring me continual refreshment.

As I type these precious moments out, I am reminded of the importance of the special things that we can give to the members of our Dream Teams. I have been blessed many times as I have helped others fulfill their dreams and have learned to sow special gifts to those people helping me as well. I have learned how refreshing, special gifts are from sharing free tickets to sporting events to delivering prepared meals to the Ground Support people who simply cheer me on from the tarmacs during my departures and arrivals.

The bottom line is that special gifts do not just happen. Giving special gifts is a result of LINK ACTIONS TO IDEAS. It starts when we keep our hearts open to thinking *Creatively Specific* so that, when we hear of an interest or an opportunity, we are positioned to pursue it beyond mere intentions. Of course, none of us are perfect (especially me). But, if we ask God for help, He will reveal the most special gift ideas to us - enabling us to bring refreshment to those amazing people in our lives.

4. Time

Quality time refreshes, so we should do ourselves a favor and spend it. Giving God our first moments of each day refreshes us in a way like nothing else can. Once God fills up our "thank tanks," we can take that refreshment and give it away.

Time is especially valuable to our families. Planned date nights with my husband are the most refreshing moments of any God-given dream that I am pursuing. Even in financially challenging times, we have always made spending quality time together a priority. I remember a time when we ate peanut butter sandwiches in the car as we drove around looking and dreaming of future real estate purchases. During this same time, my husband and I, along with our children, would meet once a week for a family picnic at a park near our church before the service. We enjoyed this time so much that we made it a regular family outing during the spring and summer months. No matter how productive our schedule may be, we have learned how refreshing spending time with one another can be and how it helps us take our God-given dream to FLIGHT.

Even when we think we do not have time, God can show us when and how to sow time. Several years back a member of one of my Dream Teams had to go in for surgery. I wanted so much to visit her but did not know how to make it work. At the time, I was homeschooling our daughter while juggling a one-year-old as well as working on ministry and writing projects. I just did not see how I was going to get over to visit this very dear person. Then God reminded me of the time I had available for breakfast. So, I called my friend and Dream Team member and proposed a plan for me and my children to bring her a homemade, hot breakfast. She was delighted. I made a quick yet yummy meal and loaded up the kids. Although we were at her house for less than an hour so as to return home and not miss a beat with our daily plan, the time that we spent was well received. My friend and family received much refreshment. When we let God guide our time, we can invest refreshment while keeping our FLIGHT plan on schedule.

5. A Simple Thank You

Giving someone thanks does not have to be a big production. What I mean is that God tells us to give, and many people do so to honor God. Our obedience does not mean that the giver would not appreciate our noticing; it does mean that the giver does not need all that and a bag of airplane pretzels just because they helped us. Writing a "thank you" note and either giving it or mailing it to a Dream Team member can refresh a person's day, week, or year. Keeping a notepad on our desks and in our briefcases, purses, and vehicles will help create an easy way for us to write to someone the moment their name crosses our heart. Sometimes, when we hesitate because we think we should do something bigger and better than writing a simple "thank you" note, we miss an opportunity to refresh.

We should not turn our THANKSGIVING into a parade; for many, just hearing the words "thank you" is an amazing gift. Whenever I was assigned territories to oversee in the business world, I would set calendar date reminders to call training managers simply to thank them for all of their hard work. Years after I had left one company, the person who took over my territory told me that people still talked about how refreshing I was - as I was the first person to call just to say thanks.

Saying "thank you" is more powerful than most people think. I remember doing some consulting for a company that had high employee turnover. A colleague and I surveyed over one hundred of their employees in one of their highest turnover areas. The data showed us that the number one complaint of working employees was the lack of verbal thanks. Don't ever underestimate the power of these two words. And, when these words are coupled with the specific detail of why we are thank-full, the recipient will be refreshed even more.

6. Finish the Work

Our God-given dreams are...well, God-given. For this reason, we give God thanks by finishing the work that He has given us. The act of finishing the work that God has given us, whatever it may be, will give God - and our Dream Team - thanks.

Our Dream Team consists of people who believe in us and the dream that God has given us and have devoted time, finances, and energy to help move that God-given dream to its destination. For this reason, our arrival is confirmation that they have been involved in the completion of something wonderful.

The Maneuver "Measure it so that we can treasure it" helps us with the Maintenance of "*Now finish the work!*" These rally calls are the motivation for our Dream Teams. When we take the time to finish the work God has given us, others will treasure the time they invested in our finished work as well.

Blessings FLIGHT Log

Keeping a close list of counted blessings along the way helps us also to "Measure it so that we can treasure it" as well as finish the work needed to fulfill our God-given dream. THANKSGIVING is not about keeping score to compare our journey with someone else's but rather helps ensure that our environment is the best that it can be. From giving to receiving, an important quality of fulfilling a God-given dream is counting our blessings.

As far as logging the blessings along our journey to our destination, we should make it easy. Whether we keep a notepad or an electronic version, we can categorize our counted blessings by month and year. Such categorization will help us see the connection between blessings and our productivity. Regularly viewing the Blessings FLIGHT Log will, in and of itself, be a blessing to us. Even during those times when we encounter turbulence, our eyes can stay focused on the good things that God is doing for and in us. We will surely treasure those things that we measure.

Encourage Yourself

God and our Dream Teams are worthy of THANKSGIVING. Yet, there is another that needs refreshment when taking a God-given dream to FLIGHT…us! Encouraging ourselves may at first seem self-serving and even somewhat prideful. With the right heart, however, it is not only important but critical to our fulfilling the plans God has for us.

Before I knew the power of the Word of God, I knew the importance of encouraging myself to keep moving a dream forward. In college, I would write desired test scores on my bathroom mirror, circle and put smiley faces next to large deposits in my checkbook ledger, and hide envelopes with small cash amounts in places I rarely frequented just to surprise myself. When I began traveling for my career, I would hide encouragement notes in suitcases and socks, and I even mailed letters to myself to hotels that I had not yet visited. Once I became a supervisor, traveling with no peers for weeks at a time, I began leaving voice mails to myself in the third person that would lift me up. During my time as a consultant, I kept a file of encouraging notes from clients who wrote to thank me and would reference this file when I needed a pick-me-up. While all this may seem excessive or even strange, I believe that had I not given myself those positive boosts, I would not have been able to keep my dreams in motion.

It is true that encouraging ourselves can help us be successful, but self-encouragement is very different from living a fulfilling life while taking God-given dreams to FLIGHT. The difference is that almost every time that I found money, heard a self-made voice message, or found a note in one of my socks - I was at the point of quitting. Sustaining myself caused for a very up and down ride along the way.

My life was like riding a roller coaster. That is until I learned what had been given to me through the Word of God. I discovered that no amount of patting myself on the back could compare to the lift that His *Wings* would give any dream that I was pursuing. The Word of God began to give me continuous refreshment. This stability change gave me a breath of fresh air and left me wanting more.

As I dug into the Scriptures, I not only learned that His plans are for me to prosper but how to encourage myself in a way that kept my focus on Him while lifting me, too. The discipline of leaving messages and notes had already been established, so all I had to do was to exchange my words for His. I began leaving myself notes and voice messages filled with encouraging and lifting Scriptures such as:

"I can do all things through Christ
who strengthens me."
(Phil. 4:13 NKJV)

"He shall be like a tree planted
by the rivers of water,

That brings forth its fruit in its season,
whose leaf also shall not wither;
And whatever he does shall prosper."
(Ps. 1:3 NKJV)
"Being confident of this very thing, that He who has begun a good work in you will complete it until the day of Jesus Christ."
(Phil. 1:6 NKJV)

"That you may walk worthy of the Lord, fully pleasing Him, being fruitful in every good work and increasing in the knowledge of God."
(Col. 1:10 NKJV)

"...for the joy of the Lord is your strength."
(Neh. 8:10 NKJV)

"For I know the plans I have for you," declares the Lord, "plans to prosper you and not to harm you, plans to give you hope and a future. Then you will call upon me and come and pray to me, and I will listen to you. You will seek me and find me when you seek me with all your heart. I will be found by you," declares the Lord.
(Jer. 29:11-14a NIV)

And, of course...

"Now finish the work, so that your eager

willingness to do it may be matched by your completion of it, according to your means. For if the willingness is there, the gift is acceptable according to what one has, not according to what he does not have."
(2 Cor. 8:11-12 NIV)

The Word of God brought **pleasure** to my pursuit. These *Wings* and many more began to change the quality of air in each God-given dream I pursued. God's Word moved me from a person who said, "Thank you" to a person who started living a life of THANKSGIVING. Not only could I encourage others, but I began to develop into a person who remained lifted - instead of the person who needed a lift as the plane appeared to be crashing. I began to live a life of **pleasure.**

The process of taking our God-given dreams to FLIGHT will not be perfect. It can, however, be thank-full and filled with refreshment, bringing **pleasure** to both us and God. Developing the *Means* of FORWARD THINKING, LINK ACTIONS TO IDEAS, INVOLVE THOSE NEEDED, GENERATE A PLAN, and HAVE ACCOUNTABILITY propels our God-given dreams towards their destinations. Yet, it is THANKSGIVING and its refreshment that fills our "thank tanks" so that we can "*Now finish the work!*" God has given us to do.

When we begin to take a God-given dream to FLIGHT, we should say with enthusiasm, "*Let's go for it!*" We should not, however, wait until we arrive to sow THANKSGIVING to all those who helped us along the way. The refreshment of THANKSGIVING comes as we develop the *Means* of FLIGHT. When we arrive at our destination, we can then say, "*Thank God we made it!*" In giving thanks, we give **pleasure** to "The One" who gave us the dream, as well as the many people who helped us fulfill it.

Let us "refresh" our memories as we review the *Means* of THANKSGIVING.

THANKSGIVING

Gate #10 - CONNECTOR QUESTION
"Who, how, and when do we give thanks?"

Maneuver: Giving Thanks to Dream Teams
Maintenance: Six Thank-Full Refreshments, Blessings FLIGHT Log, Encourage Yourself

THANKSGIVING helps us to "*Now finish the work!*" This In-FLIGHT Check will help us get to where God knows that we can be. We can enjoy and give **pleasure** to God as we…

Develop *Means* by Connecting *Wings* to God-Given Dreams

In-FLIGHT Check

Recording what we learn along the way will help us develop beyond today!

Develop *Means* of THANKSGIVING by answering this Connector Question: "Who, how, and when do we give thanks?"

Co-Pilots: ______________________________

____

____

Crew:______________________________

____

____

Passengers: ______________________________

____

____

Ground Support: ______________________________

____

____

Six Thank-Full Refreshments: Write down ideas to refresh others.

____

____

____

____

____

____

Write down a *Dated Action* to begin your Blessings FLIGHT Log:

____

____

Write down a *Dated Action* to Encourage Yourself:

____

____

Connecting *Wings* of **pleasure**: Seek God and write out Scriptures that lift the answer to the above question.

____

____

____

____

We have traveled through ***A Time to Create***,
A Time to Generate, and ***A Time to Celebrate***.
We now await our next destination!

For reapplication use printable versions
of the In-FLIGHT Check pages,
go to the link below to access these and other resources:

www.yourflightplans.com/tools

Once you have tasted flight, you will forever walk the earth
with your eyes turned skyward, for there you have been,
and there you will always ***long to return****."*

~Leonardo de Vinci

FLIGHT Pattern

God designed us to fulfill the plans that He has for us and to long to grow and develop the *Means* to do so by connecting to His *Wings*. Once we realize this, we will forever return to develop the *Means* of FLIGHT so that we can keep flying towards our next destination. Between the pages of this book are many words - God's, mine, and, hopefully, some of your own. When we connect our words with God's Word, our God-given dreams begin to emerge.

It is my hope and prayer that this book blesses us. Even more, it is my hope that it moves us to application and reapplication creating a FLIGHT Pattern. Reapplying this FLIGHT Pattern over and over will help us fulfill the plans God has for us.

Reapplication will help us arrive at our next destination.

In the beginning, I shared that FLIGHT is not about helping us discover our life-long destiny, but it will help us get there. Reapplying what we have learned through FORWARD THINKING, LINK ACTIONS TO IDEAS, INVOLVE THOSE NEEDED, GENERATE A PLAN, HAVE ACCOUNTABILITY, and THANKSGIVING to every God-given dream will create a FLIGHT Pattern. This FLIGHT Pattern will continue to develop the *Means* of FLIGHT in each of us. By reapplying the principles we have learned, it helps us connect each God-given dream to our destiny.

We should all be challenged to return to this FLIGHT Pattern of action beyond simply saying the words, "*Let's go for it!*"

The quote from Leonardo de Vinci is captivating and one of my favorites, but there is a very important piece missing - action. Without action, we remain grounded. It is when we take action that we begin to fulfill our God-given dream that will connect us to our next dream and get us to where God knows that we can be!

There will be a day when we look back on all of the God-given dreams that we have taken to FLIGHT. How awesome it will be to shout with enthusiasm, "*Thank God we made it!*" because we were willing to…

Develop *Means* by Connecting *Wings* to God-Given Dreams

FLIGHT at a Glance!

The following page is FLIGHT at a Glance! - The detailed layout of our FLIGHT Plan. This grid helps us see the big picture of FLIGHT. At ground level we take FLIGHT to action, but looking down from a thirty-thousand feet viewpoint we can see how each piece of our FLIGHT plan works together to help us reach our destination, one God-given dream at a time.

FLIGHT AT A GLANCE

Departures/ Arrivals	The Means of FLIGHT			Connector Questions	
A Time To Create	F	FORWARD THINKING	01	What is the dream and what is the point of that dream?	
			02	How do I motivate & measure my God-given dream?	
	L	LINK ACTIONS TO IDEAS	03	How do I land this plane "Creatively Specific"?	
			04	Why do it (Whatever the action is)?	
A Time To Generate	I	INVOLVE THOSE NEEDED	05	What did Air Traffic Control say?	
	G	GENERATE A PLAN	06	Why GENERATE A PLAN?	
			07	How do I pre-check the plan?	
			08	When do I just "Wing" it?	
	H	HAVE ACCOUNTABILITY	09	What is my approach?	
A Time To Celebrate	T	THANKSGIVING	10	Who, how, and when do we give thanks?	

FLIGHT AT A GLANCE

	Maneuvers & Maintenance	"Wings"
	Discover the Destination 3 R's to remember about dreams 1. Respect 2. Return 3. Reinforce	Passion & Perseverance
	Measure It So We Can Treasure "Now finish the work"	
	Bring It To The Hangar Pray, Speak, Link	
	Take Off! Link, Speak, Pray	
	Coordinates & Concordance Call, Consider, Carry	People, Planning, & Productivity
	"Wings" to God-given Dreams Connect it, don't push it	
	The 3 Pre-Check #1 Emotional Check #2 God's Plans #3 CHART the Details	
	The Power of Lift Faith in "Wings"	
	The "Up" Factor Own-Up, Know-Up, Grow-Up	
	Monday Mornings & Beyond Meetings & Mechanics	
	Giving Thanks to Dream Teams Six Thank-full Refreshments, Blessings FLIGHT Log, & Encourage Yourself	Pleasure

Forever First Class Ticket

Many of you reading this book have a vibrant relationship with God through His one Son, Jesus Christ. There are many of you, however, who might call yourself a Christian, but you do not honestly know where you will arrive on the day of your final flight. If this is you, God loves you, and He wants you to know, without a shadow of a doubt, that you can have a first class, eternal seat on His flight home. If this describes you, please read through these important boarding announcements and receive this Forever First Class Ticket.

- No matter how much baggage you may think that you have, you are accepted. And the best part is you can leave it all behind.
- Everyone boarding will be first class because your seat has been paid for at the highest price.
- There is no need to show any form of identification because God knows your name.
- There are no dress code requirements, simply come as you are.
- Seating is available to those who have made mistakes. In fact, there is nothing that you have done or that has been done to you that could disqualify you. Not perfect? WELCOME, ABOARD!
- Morally right? You may have lived a good life or consider yourself a good person, but all of us fall short

of the glory of God. This boarding call is not based on one's personal performance.

- Flying standby is not an option. You must stand up to be counted.

All metaphors aside, this is THE SINGLE MOST IMPORTANT DECISION that you will ever make. This decision will change your destiny. I know that you want to fulfill the dreams in your heart. Making a decision for Jesus Christ is the first step towards realizing them so that you can begin to fulfill them, with God's help, one dream at a time.

Obstacles will come, but with the Spirit of God living on the inside of you, hell is no longer one of those obstacles. Just like picking up this book was a choice of your free will, this, too, is a choice. So I ask you, will you humble yourself by admitting that you cannot do it alone anymore? If you believe that Jesus is "The Way" to your relationship with "The One" who created you, then confess with your mouth that Jesus is Lord of your life. Wherever you may be, right now repeat this prayer out loud, from your heart.

Father God in Jesus' name, I come to you. Sin and Satan, I turn my back to you. Father God, I turn towards you. I believe that you sent Jesus Christ to die and rise again just for me. Father God in Jesus' name, forgive me of my sins and cleanse my heart. Jesus, come into my heart and be my Lord, Savior, and Best Friend.

If you have prayed this prayer, you have just made the best decision in your life. By receiving this Forever First Class Ticket to Heaven, you also are blessed with all of God's promises through the blood of Jesus Christ. Does this mean that your life will be turbulence free? No. It means that you now have the Spirit of God living inside you to bless, heal, comfort, direct, guide, teach, and help navigate you through every God-given dream you embark on fulfilling. YOU WILL NEVER BE ALONE AGAIN. And, if you choose to dig into His Word, you will always be lifted and continue to soar higher and higher with every dream you take to FLIGHT.

The decision to make Jesus Christ your Lord is a new beginning, and all new journeys need understanding. So please get into a Bible-based church, read God's Word daily, and spend time with your Father in prayer. And remember that if you let Him, God will help you get from where you are to where He knows that you can be!

"For I know the plans I have for you," declares the Lord, "plans to prosper you and not to harm you, plans to give you hope and a future. Then you will call upon me and come and pray to me, and I will listen to you. You will seek me and find me when you seek me with all your heart. I will be found by you," declares the Lord.
(Jer. 29:11-14a NIV)

FLIGHT References

Pre-FLIGHT

1. *Means*, definition: Blue Letter Bible transliteration echo www.blueletterbible.org/lang/lexicon/lexicaon.cfm?Strongs=G2192& t=NIV (2013)

FLIGHT Plan

1. Formulate, definition: 1b www.merriam-webster.com/dictionary/ formulate (2013)

A Time To Create

1. Create, definition: 1 www.merriam-webster.com/dictionary/create (2013)

FORWARD THINKING

1. Jim Frease, Dare to Dream-How to wake up and do it. JCI, CD.
2. Reinforce, definition: 1,2,3 www.merriamwebster.com/dictionary/ reinforce (2013)
3. Hab. 2:2 NKJV

LINK ACTIONS TO IDEAS

1. Gen. 10:22 NKJV
2. Gen. 30: 25-43 NKJV
3. Prov. 1:5 NKJV
4. Deut. 28:6 NKJV
5. Hab. 2:2 NKJV

A Time To Generate

1. Generate, definition: 1b www.merriam-webster.com/dictionary/ generate (2013)

INVOLVE THOSE NEEDED

1. Matt. 6:33 NKJV
2. 2 Cor. 8:11 NKJV
3. Carry, definition: transitive verb 1 http://www.merriam-webster.com/dictionary/carry (2015)

GENERATE A PLAN

1. Plan, definition: 2a www.merriam-webster.com/dictionary/plan (2014)
2. Generate, definition: 1 www.merriam-webster.com/dictionary/generate (2014)
3. Excerpt from "The Wright Story," Brothers Aeroplaneompany/Aviation History Wing www.wright-brothers.org copyright 1999-2010
4. Reference from "1910-First 10 Women to Earn a Pilot License Worldwide," Raymonde de Laroche (France) www.centennialofwomenpilots.com (2014)
5. Reference from "Restoration: The Memphis Belle" www.airspacemag.com/military-aviation/restoration-the-memphis-belle-10460703/ (2014)
6. Reference from "The Spirit of St. Louis" www.charleslindbergh.com/plane/index.asp (2014)
7. Heb. 11:1 NKJV

HAVE ACCOUNTABILITY

1, Accountable, definition: www.merriam-webster.com/dictionary/accountability (2014)
2. Account, definition: 2a, 3a & c, 5a, 6 www.merriam-webster.com/dictionary/account (2014)
3. Ability, definition:1a & b www.merriam-webster.com/dictionary/ability (2014)
4. Transaction, definition: 1a www.merriam-webster.com/dictionary/transaction (2014)
5. Reference verse, Romans 8:1 *NKJV
6. Reference verse, Proverbs 1:5 *NKJV

A Time To Celebrate

1. Celebrate, definition: 2a www.merriam-webster.com/dictionary/celebrate (2014)

Scripture cited within the text include:

*All NKJV Scripture references taken from The Holy Bible, New King James Version Copyright 1982 by Thomas Nelson, Inc., Nashville, TN U.S.A.

*All NIV Scripture references taken from The NIV/KJV Parallel Bible, Copyright 1983 by The Zondervan Corporation, Grand Rapids, MI U.S.A.

58439162R00118

Made in the USA
Lexington, KY
10 December 2016